Shane Pruitt

REVIVAL GENERATION

AWAKENING TO A MOVEMENT OF GOD

Lifeway Press®
Brentwood, Tennessee

Publishing Team

CONTENT EDITOR
Kyle Wiltshire

DIRECTOR, STUDENT MINISTRY
Ben Trueblood

PRODUCTION EDITOR
Morgan Hawk

MANAGER, STUDENT MINISTRY PUBLISHING
Karen Daniel

GRAPHIC DESIGNERS
Shiloh Stufflebeam
Amy Lyon

Published by Lifeway Press®
©2023 Shane Pruitt
Reprinted Jan. 2024, Mar. 2024

ISBN 978-1-0877-8627-8
Item 005842565
Dewey Decimal Classification Number: 248.43
Subject Heading: RELIGION / CHRISTIAN MINISTRY / YOUTH

Printed in the United States of America.

Student Ministry Publishing
Lifeway Resources
200 Powell Place, Suite 100
Brentwood, TN 37027

We believe that the Bible has God for its author; salvation for its end; and truth, without any mixture of error, for its matter and that all Scripture is totally true and trustworthy. To review Lifeway's doctrinal guideline, please visit www.lifeway.com/doctrinalguideline.

Table of Contents

About the Author

SHANE PRUITT serves as the National Next Gen Director for the North American Mission Board (NAMB). He and his wife, Kasi, reside in Texas with their five children. He has been in ministry for more than twenty years as a denominational leader, church planter, lead pastor, and student pastor. Shane is also a traveling communicator, evangelist, and Bible teacher. Every year he speaks to over a hundred thousand people about the good news of Jesus Christ. He is the author of two books, *9 Common Lies Christians Believe: And Why God's Truth Is Infinitely Better* and *Calling Out the Called: Discipling Those Called to Ministry Leadership*, and is also one of the hosts of the GenSend Podcast. Follow him on Instagram and Twitter: @shane_pruitt78.

Introduction

Your generation is unique. You've never known a world without the internet; your parents can't say that. You've lived through a global pandemic; something you'll probably never forget. You've seen radical shifts in how society thinks, acts, and works—some good things and some not so good things.

The realities of the world you are inheriting are scary in some ways and thrilling in others. Some older folks look around and say, "What a time to be alive and young!" Some mean that in a complementary way; some don't. All this to say, the world is a complicated place right now. There are so many exciting things happening and so much that is terrifying. The question is, what will you do with the time you have?

Many of your peers will decide that they have to look out for themselves and try to make their own name great. I want to challenge you to go in a different direction. I want to challenge you to look at the world, the good and the bad, and see it through God's eyes. Every single person walking the halls of your school, every single wealthy social media influencer, every single angry person at a restaurant demanding to see the manager, every single orphan in developing countries, every single person was made in the image of God. Every single person, no matter how attractive, or poor, or intelligent, or lazy, or happy, or depressed they may be, is someone Jesus died for on the cross. I want to challenge you to live to make His name great.

You have two choices. You can sit back and let the world change around you and do nothing. Or you can say, "God, you brought me into the world at this exact moment. How do you want to use me?" You can sit in the stands and watch what God is going to do in your generation, or you can stand up, raise your hand, and echo the prophet in Isaiah 6:8 by saying, "Here am I. Send me." What a time to be alive and young! God wants to use you and your generation. I'm praying you join God in how He wants to change the world through you. I'm praying you and your entire generation will be a revival generation!

How to Use This Bible Study

This Bible study book includes eight sessions of content. Each session includes a video teaching, followed by content designed to be used by groups and individuals.

VIDEO

Each teaching video is six to eight minutes long and is designed to help introduce the main idea and engage students in discussion. There is a listening guide with blanks to fill in as students watch the video teaching. Video content can be purchased at lifeway.com/revivalgeneration.

GROUP TIME

These pages include questions and activities that guide students to respond to the video teaching and relevant Bible passages. It's important to consider the age, maturity level, and needs of students as you tailor this content to fit your group.

TIME WITH JESUS

Four days of personal study are provided for each session to take students deeper into Scripture and to further the biblical truths introduced in the group discussion and teaching time. These pages challenge students to grow in their understanding of God's Word and apply what they are learning to their everyday lives.

LEADER HELPS

At the back of the book is more content to help walk students through the material. There you will find a summary from Shane Pruitt and an icebreaker activity.

How to Access the Videos

This Bible study has eight videos—one for each session. These videos enhance the content and launch discussion.

To stream the **Revival Generation Teen Bible Study** video teaching sessions, follow these steps:

1. Purchase the group video bundle or group leader kit at lifeway.com/revivalgeneration.

2. Go to my.lifeway.com/redeem and register or log in to your Lifeway account.

3. Enter the redemption code provided at purchase to gain access to your group-use video license.

Once you've entered your personal redemption code, you can stream the video teaching sessions any time from your Digital Media page on my.lifeway.com or watch them via the Lifeway On Demand app on any TV or mobile device via your Lifeway account.

There's no need to enter your code more than once! To watch your streaming videos, just log in to your Lifeway account at my.lifeway.com or watch using the Lifeway On Demand app.

QUESTIONS? WE HAVE ANSWERS!

Visit support.lifeway.com and search "Video Redemption Code" or call our Tech Support Team at 866.627.8553.

SCAN TO
PURCHASE
THE VIDEOS

SESSION 1:
REVIVAL

IT'S MORE THAN A FEELING

Video Guide

KEY SCRIPTURE: Acts 2:42-47

1. Revival is more than a _____.

2. Revival is _____ people, who are changing their community because they're serious about the _____ of God on their lives.

3. Our nation will never experience revival until the _____ in our nation experience revival.

4. Revival always comes from God, but it comes through His _____.

"We cannot organize revival but we can set our sails to catch the wind from heaven when God chooses to blow upon His people once again."[1]

G. CAMPBELL MORGAN

"Will you not revive us again so that your people may rejoice in you."

PSALM 85:6

Group Time

IS GOD DEAD? That's what the cover read on the April 8, 1966, issue of *Time* magazine. For some, it may have felt that way. The 1960s were filled with major cultural shifts, such as rampant drug use, a sexual revolution, wars, racial unrest, political polarization, riots, protests, and attempts to tear down and rebel against traditional institutions. Sounds very similar to today, doesn't it?

What are some of the biggest issues in the world today?

People looked at everything going on in the world and began to ask questions like, "Where is God in all of this? Why isn't the church doing anything? Is there hope? Is God really dead?" Ironically, it's the same questions that many dejected people are asking today. Especially, young people. You can easily see how broken the world is. People are hurting all around us. And, deep down you want to do something about it. To put it simply, you want change.

What changes would you like to see in the world today?

Toward the end of the sixties, something shifted. It happened with young people when they began searching for hope, answers, and truth. They found that they weren't searching for something, but Someone. His name is Jesus.

A spark of revival began to grow. Within a few years, the spark turned into a raging inferno all over the United States and beyond. One scholar, who studied this movement of God, estimated that well over a quarter of a million new young people began to follow Jesus during these years.[2] This revival came to be known as the Jesus Movement or the Jesus Revolution. Even *Time* magazine noticed. On June 21, 1971, just five short years after their "Is God Dead?" cover, *Time's* new cover read: "The Jesus Revolution."

Now, it's time to ask God to do it again. It's time for revival.

When you hear the word revival, what do you think of?

REVIVAL is the awakening of God's people to their true purpose. Revival occurs when the Holy Spirit empowers and inspires people to get serious about knowing Jesus and obeying the Scriptures.

Many people think that revival is a feeling, your emotions are stirred up with lots of crying and "Holy Spirit goosebumps." Of course, tears may be involved, but true revival is God's people getting serious about worshiping Him above all and living out their true purpose of knowing Him and making Him known.

Revival is more than a feeling; it's an awakening.

What would it take for revival to happen again?

Do you believe that this generation of teens and young adults, your generation, could be known as the Revival Generation?

BELIEVE IT & LIVE IT

To look forward, we first need to look back. Let's go back to when the church got started. Jesus, the Son of God, who has always existed, took a mission trip from heaven to earth to become a man and died for the sins of all humanity. However, He never stopped being God. Fully God, fully man, He lived the perfect life that you and I couldn't live—a sin-free life. He took our place on the cross as a perfect substitute and sacrifice, paying the debt for our sin. The Savior died there on that cross and was buried in a borrowed tomb, but on the third day He overcame the grave and rose again. Then, look what He did:

> After he had suffered, he also presented himself alive to them
> by many convincing proofs, appearing to them over a period of forty
> days and speaking about the kingdom of God. **ACTS 1:3**

On the fortieth day, the last thing Jesus told His followers before He ascended back to heaven was a beautiful promise, but it's also a guiding statement for what they were supposed to do with their lives from that point forward.

> "But you will receive power when the Holy Spirit has come
> on you, and you will be my witnesses in Jerusalem, in all Judea
> and Samaria, and to the ends of the earth." **ACTS 1:8**

The promise of the Holy Spirit is a beautiful promise. Here is the Son of God promising the Spirit of God to be given to all believers. When you receive His Spirit, you will also receive His power, and this power will launch you to live differently everywhere you go.

From this timeline of the birth of the church, what stands out as most significant to you?

In Acts 2, you see the promise is fulfilled. The Spirit of God came to dwell and remain inside of Jesus's disciples, and He changed everything. Peter (who just a few days before, denied knowing Jesus three different times) was now standing before thousands of people boldly sharing the gospel.

> Peter replied, "Repent and be baptized, each of you, in the
> name of Jesus Christ for the forgiveness of your sins, and you
> will receive the gift of the Holy Spirit." **ACTS 2:38**

What happened next is where we can trace our roots back to as the New Testament church.

> So those who accepted his message were baptized, and that day
> about three thousand people were added to them. **ACTS 2:41**

That is a lot of men, women, boys, and girls who were filled with the Holy Spirit and began a new way of life. Those changed lives went on to change their communities. **This is what revival looks like!**

Has there been a time in your life when you repented of your sins and placed your faith in Jesus Christ as Lord and Savior? If so, have you been baptized? Why or why not?

Make a list of five things the disciples did in Acts 2:42-47 that revealed their changed lives.

1.   2.   3.

4.   5.

Wow! That sounds exciting, doesn't it? That is definitely a community I would want to be a part of. How about you?

Revival is the overwhelming power of the Holy Spirit that fills us with such awe that we can't help but start living differently. When God's people live differently, everything around them is affected.

HOW DO WE EXPERIENCE REVIVAL?

You can't manipulate or force revival to happen. Ultimately, revival is a work of God and only comes from His Spirit. However, we can be prepared if God so chooses to bring revival.

> **Do you think there are times when God is ready to bring revival to His people, but we're not prepared, so we miss it? Why?**

> **In Acts 2:2, the Bible describes the Spirit as a "rushing wind." How do we prepare ourselves to catch the wind from heaven if God chooses to send it?**

First of all, you must have the Holy Spirit. In Acts 2, it was the people who had the Holy Spirit that experienced the power of God.

How do you know if you have the Holy Spirit living inside of you?

We know we have the Holy Spirit if we have genuinely placed our faith in Jesus as Lord and Savior. Has there ever been a time in your life when you truly believed the gospel and placed your faith in Jesus as Lord and Savior of your life? If not, right now is the time to do that.

> If you confess with your mouth, "Jesus is Lord," and believe in your heart that God raised him from the dead, you will be saved.
> **ROMANS 10:9**

From the list you created using Acts 2:42-47, what do you see revealed in your life right now?

What are some things that are absent but should be there?

Revival is more than a feeling. It's a movement of God. Take the next four days to go deeper into what revival is and spend some time with Jesus.

NEW BELIEVER RESOURCES

If you've placed your faith in Jesus for the first time today, the Holy Spirit now lives in you. Yes, you! But this is just the first step. Two great resources for students who recently started following Jesus are:

Life Essentials: A Digital New Beginners Guide for Students

(Get FREE access to next steps videos by texting LIFE to 888-123)

Follower: Beginning Your Walk with Jesus

by Lifeway Students

REVIVAL IS BEING FILLED WITH THE HOLY SPIRIT

READ JOHN 3:5-8.

"Bless your heart" is a statement used in the southern part of the United States, often as a passive aggressive way of implicating that what the person said or did wasn't necessarily the smartest thing in the world. Personally, I feel like I've had this said to me by friends and family way too many times to count. I tend to specialize in saying things that sound a lot better in my head than they do coming out of my mouth.

A man named Nicodemus had one of those moments with Jesus. However, thankfully, Jesus is a lot more patient and kind than we tend to be. Basically, Jesus told Nicodemus (who was a very religious man) that he must be born again to see the kingdom of God (v. 3). It's a great reminder that being religious and moral does not save you. We all desperately need a Savior.

Interestingly, Nicodemus was only thinking purely in physical terms, "How can anyone be born when he is old?" (v. 4). This is probably the part where the rest of us would have said, "Nicodemus, bless your heart." However, Jesus responded that being a part of the family of God is not something you're physically born into; it's something you have to be spiritually reborn into. You must be born of the Spirit. You must have "two births": a physical birth (born of the flesh) and a spiritual birth (born of the Spirit).

Revival is more than a feeling; it's being filled with the Holy Spirit.

Have you had two births? Of course, we've all had a physical birth, but have you also have a spiritual birth?

Write down your physical birthday. If you remember when it was, also write down your spiritual birthday. (Maybe even write it in your Bible. It's an extremely important day!)

In John 3:8, Jesus compared the Spirit to the wind. We also saw that comparison in Acts 2. I can't help but think of G. Campbell Morgan's quote:

"We cannot organize revival, but we can set our sails to catch the wind from heaven when God chooses to blow upon His people once again."[3]

One of the best ways to "set your sails to catch the wind from heaven" and experience revival is by praying. Talking to God, listening to what He has to say to you, and thinking about who He is and the promises of His Scriptures.

PRAYER MOVEMENTS

HANDS UP
A sign of surrender.

- **Read Colossians 1:16.**

Spend time telling God how great He is. Not because He needs to hear it but because you need to be reminded. **Surrender** to the truth of who He is today and that He is worth following.

HANDS OPEN
A sign of emptying out.

- **Read Matthew 16:24.**

What do you need to let go of today? What is getting in the way of you going all in on following Jesus, or what is tripping you up as you follow Him? **Empty out** by confessing any unrepentant sin.

HANDS OUT
A sign of receiving.

- **Read Proverbs 3:5-6.**

Lastly, ask God to be with you today. Let Him know you are ready to **receive** any truth He teaches you. Through the power of the Holy Spirit be ready to obey anything He calls you to today. You're ready to receive His orders for you.

REVIVAL IS A REMINDER OF YOUR IDENTITY IN CHRIST

September 18, 2004, the day I got married, is the day that my identity completely changed. Sure, I still have the same name and the same DNA, but I am no longer the same. Where I was once single, I am now a husband. It's a new identity.

As a husband there is now an expectation for me to live differently than when I was single. A new identity (being a husband) now requires new activity (living like a husband).

Revival is more than a feeling; it's a reminder of your identity in Christ.

What significant event in your life do you feel changed you? How did it begin to make you live differently?

That is what it means to follow Jesus as a born-again child of the most high God. In the moment that you were bought by the blood of Jesus and the Holy Spirit came to live inside of you, your identity changed. Yes, you still have the same name and the same DNA, but something radically changed for you that day!

READ COLOSSIANS 3:1-4.

This is exactly what Paul was talking about in Colossians 3:1-4. In verse 1, you see the work of the gospel changing who you are. The old you (a sinner separated from God) has died, and now a new you has "been raised with Christ" (Col. 3:1). When the power of God changes your *identity*, it will also begin to change your *activity*.

Are there any actions or habits you continue to commit that no longer fit your identity in Christ? Make a list.

Take those to the Lord right now in prayer, confessing and surrendering them over to Him. The gospel has already given you the power of victory, so by faith, it is time to trust that power by living differently.

PRAYER MOVEMENTS

HANDS UP
A sign of surrender.

- **Read 1 Timothy 1:17.**

Spend time giving glory to God. Think about all the ways He is wonderful and awesome and tell Him. **Surrender** anything inside of you that wants to keep the glory for yourself and give it to Him.

HANDS OPEN
A sign of emptying out.

- **Read Matthew 16:25.**

What do you need to lose today? What needs to go so that you can find your identity only in Him? **Empty out** by confessing anything you are holding on to, or any notion that you can save yourself in your own power.

HANDS OUT
A sign of receiving.

- **Read Philippians 2:1-4.**

Lastly, ask God to help you **receive** the blessing and calling of having the same attitude as Jesus and placing others before yourself.

> # REVIVAL IS REALIZING THAT JESUS IS THE MOST VALUABLE TREASURE OF ALL

I love shoes. I'm what some people would call a sneaker head. However, there is one pair of shoes I'll never own: The solid gold OVO x Air Jordan 10s. According to Luxe Digital, they're solid twenty-four carat gold, worth two million dollars, and weigh fifty pounds each![4]

What is the most valuable thing you own? How did you obtain it?

READ MATTHEW 13:44-46.

No matter how valuable these things are, nothing even comes close to the value of having a relationship with King Jesus. In these two parables, Jesus compared the kingdom of heaven to two treasures. The first parable compared the kingdom of heaven to a treasure found in a field. The man who found it sold everything he had to buy the field, so he could have the valuable treasure. The second parable compared the kingdom of heaven to a pearl of great price. The pearl merchant also sold all he had to buy this great pearl. What was Jesus saying in these two parables? Receiving the kingdom of God is nothing less than exchanging all that you are for all that He is.

Revival is more than a feeling; it's realizing that Jesus is the most valuable treasure of all.

Why are we tempted to treasure things more than Jesus?

You cannot hold on to the things of God and to the things of this world at the same time. You must let go of one or the other. Only the kingdom of God will last forever. The things of the world are passing away. Don't let the most glorious treasure slip away for lesser, corruptible disappointments.

What are some things or people in your life that you are currently valuing more than Jesus?

Take several minutes and listen to your favorite worship song right now. Don't hesitate to sing along with it and worship Jesus for the treasure that He is. Be reminded that He is the most valuable treasure of all.

PRAYER MOVEMENTS

HANDS OPEN
A sign of emptying out.

- **Read Hebrews 4:12.**

Grasp the reality of the treasure that is God's Word. **Empty out** by letting His truth enter your soul and judge the thoughts and intentions of your heart.

HANDS UP
A sign of surrender.

- **Read 2 Samuel 7:22.**

Be like David today and tell God how great He is. Remind yourself that there is no one like Him. **Surrender** to Him and know that He is worth following with your whole heart.

HANDS OUT
A sign of receiving.

- **Read John 3:16.**

Know with everything in you that God loves you. He loves you so much He sent His Son to die for you. **Receive** the treasure of the salvation He offers us all in Jesus and go in any direction He gives you today.

REVIVAL IS A CALLING TO INFLUENCE THOSE AROUND YOU

READ MATTHEW 5:13-16.

The power of the gospel not only saves you *from* things, it also saves you *to* things. Often, we focus on how the gospel saves us from things like sin, death, destruction, and hell—and all of that is true. However, we also need to start focusing more on how the gospel calls us to things like a relationship with a risen King, a church family, a kingdom, and a mission to make Jesus known.

List below three things God is calling you from and calling you to:

There are many Christians who believe that they are to separate themselves from the world completely. They feel that the more they hide themselves, the more spiritual they become. In fact, many churches have come to adopt this same mentality. Sadly, many churches have become like private little clubs.

Why does reaching people different from us often intimidate us?

Jesus taught that we are not to separate ourselves from the world. We are to engage and influence our country and the towns we live in. Jesus implored His followers to be salt and light. We need followers of Christ who are not scared to have God shine through them so brightly that they affect the world around them.

Revival is more than a feeling; it's a calling to influence those around you.

Real revival will launch us into the world to live differently, to love people, to serve, and to point others to Jesus.

Name specific areas in your life where God is calling you to be "salt" and "light." (For example, in your school, sports teams, family, job, etc.)

PRAYER MOVEMENTS

HANDS UP
A sign of surrender.

- **Read John 4:24.**

Spend time praying and referring to God by some of His names from Scripture, like Redeemer, Immanuel, Wonderful Counselor, and so on. Not because He needs to be reminded of His names but because you need to be reminded. **Surrender** to the truth of who He is today and that He is worth following.

HANDS OPEN
A sign of emptying out.

- **Read 1 John 1:9-10.**

What do you need to let go of today? Is there unconfessed sin that you've been holding on to? The gospel is also a calling to obedience and holiness. **Empty out** by giving it to your heavenly Father. Let Him handle it. When you get serious about wanting revival, you'll also need to be serious about keeping away from sin.

HANDS OUT
A sign of receiving.

- **Read Acts 1:8.**

Ask God to remind you of His power today. God has called you to be a witness and to make Him known to the ends of the earth. He has given you the power to do just that, which is His Holy Spirit. Let Him know you're ready to **receive** this calling through His power today.

SESSION 2: WORSHIP

IT'S MORE THAN A SONG

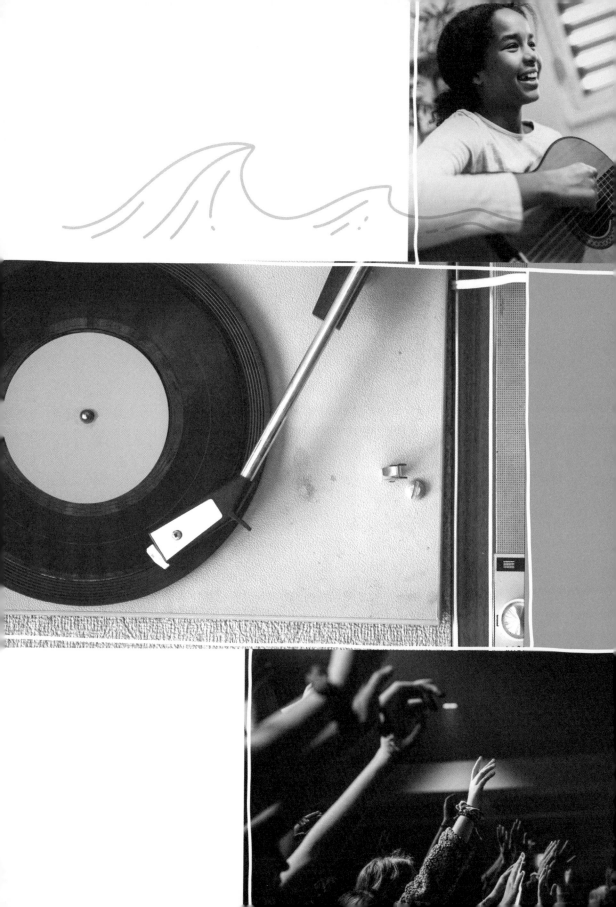

Video Guide

KEY SCRIPTURE: Jeremiah 10:1-6

1. Worship is more than a song. Worship is a _____.

> "The human heart is a factory of idols. Everyone of us is, from his mother's womb, expert in inventing idols."[1]
>
> JOHN CALVIN

2. _____ that we worship other than Jesus is an idol, and it will never fulfill us.

3. You'll always feel like something is missing in your life as long as _____ is missing—God Almighty.

4. We have a lot more time than we realize; we just _____ it on lesser important things.

5. Revival takes place when you're willing to _____ _____ your idols because you realize _____ is better than anything the world has to offer.

Group Time

CLEAR THE STAGE. One of my all-time favorite worship songs is called "Clear the Stage" by a worship leader named Ross King. The song is over twenty years old, but look up the lyrics and see how relevant they still are.

> When you hear the word worship, what do tend to think of?

Most often when we hear the word *worship*, we think of music. We probably envision people lifting their hands while singing along with a worship band. Obviously, worshiping God through music is a form of worship. However, like Ross King stated, "worship is more than a song."[2]

WORSHIP is placing your highest adoration and affection on someone or something. Basically, whatever or whomever is most important in your life is what or who you're worshiping.

> Who or what are some things we tend to worship in the world today?

According to the Bible, anything or anyone that we worship that is not God is actually considered an idol. In fact, the first two commandments of the Ten Commandments address idolatry.

READ EXODUS 20:1-4.

Revival, or a movement of God in our lives, will stir us to lay down our idols and worship God alone.

BELIEVE IT & LIVE IT

¹ Hear the word that the LORD has spoken to you, house of Israel. ² This is what the LORD says: Do not learn the way of the nations or be terrified by signs in the heavens, although the nations are terrified by them, ³ for the customs of the peoples are worthless. Someone cuts down a tree from the forest; it is worked by the hands of a craftsman with a chisel. ⁴ He decorates it with silver and gold. It is fastened with hammer and nails, so it won't totter. ⁵ Like scarecrows in a cucumber patch, their idols cannot speak. They must be carried because they cannot walk. Do not fear them for they can do no harm—and they cannot do any good. ⁶ LORD, there is no one like you. You are great; your name is great in power. ⁷ Who should not fear you, King of the nations? It is what you deserve. For among all the wise people of the nations and among all their kingdoms, there is no one like you. ⁸ They are both stupid and foolish, instructed by worthless idols made of wood! ⁹ Beaten silver is brought from Tarshish and gold from Uphaz. The work of a craftsman and of a goldsmith's hands is clothed in blue and purple, all the work of skilled artisans. ¹⁰ But the LORD is the true God; he is the living God and eternal King. The earth quakes at his wrath, and the nations cannot endure his fury. **JEREMIAH 10:1-10**

Jeremiah, who many call the weeping prophet, was a young man sent by God to His people. He passionately pleaded with the Israelites to turn toward the Lord with humility and repentance to avoid God's judgment against them. Originally, God had set apart this chosen nation (the Israelites) to worship Him above all and to live differently than all the other nations. The purpose was that God's children would live and act so differently that everyone else would see their lifestyles and customs and be drawn to their God. Then, the Israelites would point these other nations to the true and living God, who would be ready to welcome them to worship Him, as well.

However, time and time again, instead of the Israelites influencing other nations, they would be influenced by their neighbors. In fact, they began to worship the idols of these other nations. God speaks about this very thing through Jeremiah in the verses we just read. Read back over Jeremiah 10:1-10, and let's discuss these two questions together:

In Jeremiah 10:1-10, what does the Bible say about idols?

In Jeremiah 10:1-10, what does the Bible say about the Lord?

When we think of idols, we may picture the literal idols described by Jeremiah—little statues created by human hands adorned with jewelry. However, idols can take on many shapes and expressions. Even today, we still tend to worship created things; they have just been modernized—cell phones, sports, social media, video games, ourselves, a boyfriend or girlfriend, our popularity, our looks, and the list goes on and on.

No one literally bows down and worships their phone, sports team, or video games (at least, I hope not), but how do we still worship these things?

HOW DO WE WORSHIP LIKE WE WERE CREATED TO?

First of all, we have to realize that worship is natural to us. God created each of us to be worshipers. It's your purpose in life to worship. In fact, you don't even have to learn how to worship. You didn't have to take a class or have a lesson on how to worship. You can't help but worship. We all long to offer our highest affections to something or someone.

The question is not if you're worshiping—you are. The question is always, "Who or what are you worshiping?" If it's not Jesus, your heart will always seek to worship other things.

> "The human heart is a factory of idols.
> Every one of us is, from his mother's womb,
> expert in inventing idols."[3]
>
> JOHN CALVIN

However, we were not created by God to worship other things or people; we were created by God to worship Him alone.

The people I formed for myself will declare my praise. **ISAIAH 43:21**

Let's answer some rapid fire questions:

Who did God form?

Who does God have a plan and purpose for?

Who is, from birth, able to worship?

The answer to all three of these questions is *everyone*! God made everyone, has a plan and purpose for everyone, and everyone is born a worshiper. Earlier, we considered what we tend to worship over God. Now, let's make it more personal.

What has to happen in your life to shift your worship of these other things to God?

You may think a particular idol will eventually make you feel whole inside.

"If I could just make the varsity team . . ."

"If I could just get that person that I am crushing on to like me back . . ."

"If I could just get enough followers on social media . . ."

" . . . then, I would be complete."

Really?

The truth is that as soon as you achieve these things, something else will rise up and replace it. You'll always feel like something is missing as long as Someone is missing—His name is Jesus.

Personal revival is experienced when you're willing to do what the song *"Clear the Stage"* said and clear the stage of your heart to make space for the only one who deserves it. May Jesus be the One who is center stage of your heart through the power of the Holy Spirit.

What practical action steps do you need to take this week to make sure Jesus is center stage of your heart and not idols?

[WORSHIP IS LAYING DOWN OUR IDOLS]

READ 1 SAMUEL 5:1-4.

In this passage, the ark of God has been taken by the Philistines after defeating the Israelites in battle. What is the ark of God? A symbol of the presence of God with His people here on earth. Also known as the ark of the covenant, it was a constant reminder of the promise God made with His people to be their God.

Dagon was a half-human/half-fish god of fertility that the Philistines worshiped. Worship and sacrifices were made in the temple of Dagon where the massive statue was found.

When you read this account in 1 Samuel, who do you think won this match between God and Dagon? Why?

God knocked the statue (idol) to the ground, and the priests had to help it back up. Then, God destroyed the idol by breaking it. I think it's pretty clear who the victor was. In our lives, God will sometimes knock over or break our idols, so we can clearly see and truly worship Him.

Has there been a time when God had to knock down an idol in your life? What happened?

We often have a choice—we can either lay down our idols voluntarily, or He will knock them down forcefully. This is out of His incredible love and goodness toward us, because our Creator is truly better than any idol.

Worship is more than a song; it's laying down our idols.

Like the people standing Dagon back up, what are some idols you're always tempted to stand back up after laying them down?

Laying down idols is not a one-time act; it is a daily discipline. We're always tempted to stand them back up. The best way to daily lay down idols or keep them down is to stay close to God through Scripture and prayer.

PRAYER MOVEMENTS

HANDS UP
A sign of surrender.

- **Read Psalm 150:6.**

Spend time worshiping God. You need to be reminded daily that He is God, and He is worthy of worship. **Surrender** to the truth of who He is today and that He is worth worshiping.

HANDS OPEN
A sign of emptying out.

- **Read 1 John 5:21.**

What do you need to lay down today? What is getting in the way of you seeing your Savior clearly? What needs to be knocked over or broken because it's stealing your worship away from Him? **Empty out** by confessing any idols.

HANDS OUT
A sign of receiving.

- **Read Jonah 2:8.**

Ask God to overwhelm you with His love today. Let Him know you are ready to **receive** it fully. Through the power of the Holy Spirit be ready to abandon your idols because you know His faithful love is better.

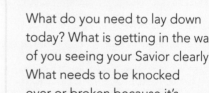

[WORSHIP IS A REMINDER OF HOW AWESOME GOD IS]

READ PSALM 139:7-10.

One of God's attributes is that He is omnipresent, which means that He is everywhere. This is difficult for us to understand because we're always trapped by location. You can't physically be in two places at once. This does not apply to God. He is everywhere at once. His presence fills all of creation. He truly is an awesome God!

Where are some places that you've traveled to?

The reality of God's omnipresence can be both comforting and convicting. It's comforting because you're never alone. Maybe you feel like you're the only authentic follower of Jesus at your school, in your family, or in your circle of friends. However, you're never alone. God is always with you. He is with you at school, at home, at the mall, everywhere, and He will never leave you.

Read Deuteronomy 31:6 and fill in the blanks.

"Be strong and_____; don't be terrified or afraid of them. For the _____ your _____ is the one who will go with you; he will not _____ you or _____ you."

The omnipresence of God can also be convicting. Have you ever asked yourself, "Would I be doing this, watching this, or saying this right now if God was here?" Guess what? He is. God is always there. The presence of His holiness should compel us toward holiness.

Worship is more than a song; it's a reminder of how awesome He is.

When you remember how awesome the Lord is, this is will cultivate an attitude of continual worship of Him in you. Your awesome God is always with you, so you should seek to always worship Him.

Is the omnipresence of God more comforting or convicting to you? Why do you feel that way?

Whether you're comforted or convicted by God's awesome presence, now is the perfect time to take these feelings to Him.

PRAYER MOVEMENTS

HANDS UP
A sign of surrender.

- **Read Psalm 95:6.**

God is your maker. Worship Him today. **Surrender** to the truth of how awesome He is and that He is worth following.

HANDS OPEN
A sign of emptying out.

- **Read John 16:7-8.**

What is the awesome presence of God convicting you of today? **Empty out** by confessing anything that is not pleasing to the God whom you've been called to worship.

HANDS OUT
A sign of receiving.

- **Read 2 Corinthians 1:3.**

Don't forget that your awesome God is with you today. Let Him know you are ready to **receive** His comfort, and through the power of the Spirit, you're ready to obey anything He calls you to because you know He is with you.

WORSHIP IS TRUSTING IN THE POWER OF GOD

READ MARK 2:9-12.

Have you ever heard the old cliché "actions speak louder than words"? Personally, if someone tells me they can do something, that's fine, but I want to see them do it.

> What has someone claimed they could do, but it seemed so unbelievable that you challenged them to prove it?

> What is your rare talent or true story that people have a hard time believing?

Jesus was faced with this challenge constantly. However, unlike us, He was able to do what He said He could do every single time without fail.

In Mark 2, a paralyzed man dropped through the roof into Jesus's lap. Knowing that the man's spiritual sickness was of more importance than his physical condition, Christ decided to heal his soul first. However, the scribes within the crowd silently questioned this, "Who can forgive sins but God alone?" (v. 7).

Then, the Son of God did something that gave action to His ability to forgive sins. He showed the crowd a miracle that they could see, so they could believe in His ability to perform miracles that they couldn't see.

> What is something that God has done in your life that seems unbelievable to others?

If Jesus has forgiven you of your sins, that is an absolute miracle in itself. Salvation is a miraculous work of an all-powerful God.

Worship is more than a song; it's trusting in the power of God.

God is truly all-powerful and one hundred percent worthy of your worship. However, it is so easy to forget how powerful our God is because life's circumstances can seem so powerful and overwhelming.

What circumstance in your life right now seems bigger than God's power?

One of the reasons you need prayer and Scripture reading every day is because that time with the Lord is a great reminder of who He is and how Jesus is always bigger than your circumstances.

PRAYER MOVEMENTS

HANDS UP
A sign of surrender.

- **Read Exodus 15:6.**

Spend time reflecting on how powerful your great God is. You don't worship a weak God; you worship an all-powerful God. **Surrender** to the truth of who He is today and that His power can sustain you and break the enemy.

HANDS OPEN
A sign of emptying out.

- **Read Psalm 27:1.**

Is there someone or something you are fearing or dreading today? **Empty out** by trusting in the power of the Lord who is your salvation. Let Him handle the situation that you're dreading.

HANDS OUT
A sign of receiving.

- **Read Isaiah 41:10.**

Ask God to remind you of His power today. Let Him know you are ready to **receive** the promise that He is holding you with His righteous right hand. You're ready to receive any direction He carries you toward today.

WORSHIP IS A LIFESTYLE

"What time does worship start? When is it over?" How many times have we asked these questions or something similar? Now, I realize that we are typically talking about church service times when we ask these questions. So, we usually respond with, "Worship starts at 10:30 a.m., and it ends when the pastor stops preaching. Hopefully, it's early enough to beat all the crowds from all the other churches to the restaurants." Maybe, that is just me!

What is your favorite restaurant?

READ ROMANS 12:1-2.

In Romans 12, Paul urged believers to present themselves "as a living sacrifice . . . this is your true worship (v. 1)." Another way to say it: worship is a lifestyle. When does the worship of Jesus start? At salvation. When is worship over? Never! You are now called to worship Jesus twenty-four hours a day, seven days a week. Everywhere you go on any day of the week, you are called to worship Jesus.

How does this truth change your view of worship?

Some people have rightfully pointed out that worshiping Jesus at church is easy. But what about living a lifestyle of worship at school, on your sports team, at the movies, and at your house? If followers of Jesus truly lived lifestyles of worshiping Him, this would change our schools, our communities, and our nation.

Worship is more than a song; it's a lifestyle.

In what areas of your life do you have the hardest time worshiping Jesus?

The truth is you will never publicly live a lifestyle of worshiping Jesus, if you don't live a lifestyle of worshiping Jesus privately through Scripture and prayer. The power to publicly display worship will only come from an overflow of privately worshiping Him.

PRAYER MOVEMENTS

HANDS UP
A sign of surrender.

- **Read Matthew 6:33.**

Worshiping Jesus as a lifestyle is seeking Him above all things at all times. Spend time praying to God and asking Him to give you the daily perspective that His kingdom is always worth seeking above everything else. **Surrender** to the truth of what His kingdom is today.

HANDS OPEN
A sign of emptying out.

- **Read Romans 1:25.**

What worship do you need to let go of today? Do you tend to worship created things instead of the Creator Himself? **Empty out** by placing proper worship on the One who deserves it. When you get serious about right worship, you'll also be in a serious spot to experience personal revival.

HANDS OUT
A sign of receiving.

- **Read Matthew 19:26.**

Ask God to remind you of His power today. Receive the truth that God has called you to live a lifestyle of worship. You're not worshiping a weak God but an all-powerful God, and nothing is impossible for Him. Let Him know you're ready to **receive** this lifestyle through His power today.

SESSION 3:
REPENTANCE

IT'S MORE THAN APOLOGIZING TO GOD

Video Guide

KEY SCRIPTURE: ACTS 19:17-20

1. Repentance is not just apologizing to God. It's really a

   _____ lifestyle.

2. When God changes your heart and mind, He will also change

   your _____.

3. Two Kinds of Repentance in the Bible:

   • Repentance unto the Lord for _____.

   • Daily _____.

4. Revival takes place when God begins to change you: your _____ ,

   your _____ , and your _____.

> "Revival begins when you draw a circle
> around yourself and make sure everything
> in that circle is right with God."[1]
>
> ANNE GRAHAM LOTZ

Group Time

REVIVAL AT THE DUMPSTERS. It was a Saturday night in West Texas where I had just preached on what biblical repentance looks like in the Scriptures. Then, the Holy Spirit did what only He can do; He changed the hearts and minds of the students. They wanted to know and follow Him so closely that they were willing to get rid of anything that was going to hinder their relationship with God. It truly was one of those special nights where hundreds of teenagers were on their faces praying, weeping, and confessing their sin before God. After some time, the response went from teens apologizing to God in tears to taking actual steps toward life change. Students began telling their leaders about things in their cars that they knew weren't pleasing to God, and they wanted to get rid of them immediately.

For well over an hour, a line of cars pulled up to the dumpsters, and one by one, items were thrown away. This response went on for the next several days, as leaders and parents went so far as to help students return merchandise that they had stolen from stores and their schools. It was a real revival of repentance!

What comes to mind when you hear the word repentance?

When you hear the word repentance you might think of confessing sin or apologizing to God. Certainly, confessing sin and apologizing to God is part of it. However, biblical repentance is much more than those two things. It's impossible to have revival without true repentance.

REPENTANCE is rooted in the Greek word *metanoia*, which is a change of mind and a change of heart that will lead to a change in lifestyle.

There are two forms of repentance in the Bible: 1) The initial repenting of sin at salvation, and 2) the lifestyle of repentance that comes with following Jesus. As you follow Jesus daily, the Holy Spirit changes your heart and mind to see sin the way your heavenly Father does. This requires repentance as you grow in Him.

Why is continued repentance necessary if you've already been saved and forgiven of your sins at salvation?

Revival is often preceded by repentance. When God changes our hearts and minds, He will also change our actions.

BELIEVE IT & LIVE IT

Unfortunately, it's often easy to confuse false repentance for real repentance. It can be best described as the differences in a fan and a follower of Jesus. Kyle Idleman in his book, *Not a Fan*, says, "The biggest threat to the church today is fans who call themselves Christians but aren't actually interested in following Christ. They want to be close enough to Jesus to get all the benefits, but not so close that it requires anything from them."[2]

Fans of Jesus: Fans acts as fans at sporting events do. They're not really in the game; they're in the stands eating nachos. They respect the game, but they keep their distance. Fans of Jesus do the same thing. They may say they respect and believe in Jesus, but they keep their distance. They don't want Him leading or changing their lives. But Jesus doesn't say, "Come and fan-boy Me." His invitation is to come and follow Him (see Matt. 4:19).

Followers of Jesus: Followers of Jesus are all in. They realize that Jesus must be Savior *and* Lord. They're up close and personal with Him. He is their life. By faith and repentance, they're willing to get rid of anything that stands in the way of becoming more like Him. Also, by the power of Holy Spirit through repentance, they're willing to remove anything in their lives that is going to trip them up as they follow Him.

What would be an example of false repentance as opposed to true repentance?

> [11] God was performing extraordinary miracles by Paul's hands, [12] so that even facecloths or aprons that had touched his skin were brought to the sick, and the diseases left them, and the evil spirits came out of them. [13] Now some of the itinerant Jewish exorcists also attempted to pronounce the name of the Lord Jesus over those who had evil spirits, saying, "I command you by the Jesus that Paul preaches!" [14] Seven sons of Sceva, a Jewish high priest, were doing this. [15] The evil spirit answered them, "I know Jesus, and I recognize Paul—but who are you?" [16] Then the man who had the evil spirit jumped on them, overpowered them all, and prevailed against them, so that they ran out of that house naked and wounded. [17] When this became known to everyone who lived in Ephesus, both Jews and Greeks, they became afraid, and the name of the Lord Jesus was held in high esteem. [18] And many who had become believers came confessing and disclosing their practices, [19] while many of those who had practiced magic collected their books and burned them in front of everyone. So they calculated their value and found it to be fifty thousand pieces of silver. [20] In this way the word of the Lord spread and prevailed. **ACTS 19:11-20**

In Acts 19:11-20, you see an example of a true follower of Jesus in Paul, and you see examples of fans in the sons of Sceva.

> **What are some of the major differences in Paul and the sons of Sceva?**

Paul, as a follower of Jesus, was all in. God does extraordinary things through ordinary people who have had a true change of heart and mind (repentance). Some people may object saying that Paul was an apostle who wrote two-thirds of the New Testament. Of course, God would use him. He was a super-Christian, right? But don't forget who Paul was before he met Jesus and had a true repentance experience through the power of the Holy Spirit. His name was Saul. Saul persecuted the church. He oversaw the death and imprisonment of Christians. If God can change and use Paul, He can change and use you.

The seven sons of Sceva were traveling exorcists. These seven brothers would find someone who was demon-possessed and, for a sum of money, would try to cast out the demon by prayers and chants. They would even sell trinkets to scare off evil spirits. For these brothers, it was a business. However, they'd heard about Jesus through the ministry of Paul. When they saw the power associated with Jesus, they wanted some of it for themselves. So, they began to use the name of Jesus as a part of their business plan. They didn't know Jesus or worship Him. They had become fans.

What are some real-life examples of the differences between fans of Jesus and followers of Jesus today?

What keeps fans of Jesus from going all out and genuinely following Him?

In Acts 19:17-20, you see many people in Ephesus experience true repentance. The evidence of this was the change that happened in their lifestyles.

HOW DO WE LIVE A LIFESTYLE OF REPENTANCE?

And many who had become believers came confessing
and disclosing their practices. **ACTS 19:18**

The people of Ephesus realized Jesus was truly better than anything they had invested their lives in before. They wanted to know Him, love Him, and worship Him above all, so everything that was going to hinder that had to go.

Quietly consider this question: Am I a follower of Jesus or just a fan? Then, answer this question: Why is being a follower of Jesus better than being a fan?

> "Revival begins when you draw a circle around yourself and make sure everything in that circle is right with God."[3]
>
> ANNE GRAHAM LOTZ

Reflect on the Anne Graham Lotz quote above. What inside your circle, through the power of the Holy Spirit, needs to be made right with God?

A lifestyle of repentance is a moment by moment realization that Jesus is better than anything that may trip you up as you follow Him. When temptation comes, remember in that moment that Jesus is better. Eventually, moments will turn into years of following Jesus. It doesn't mean that you will be perfect, but you will be made different because the Spirit inside you will be daily changing your heart and mind to be more like Jesus.

[REPENTANCE IS BELIEVING THAT JESUS IS BETTER]

Before you get to the main matchup of any boxing event, there are always undercard bouts. Undercard bouts are often fights between two lesser-known boxers designed to get the crowd ready for the big fight they all came to see. Maybe you're not a boxing fan, but you are a foodie. When you go to a restaurant there are appetizers that serve as preparation for the main course.

What is your favorite appetizer to eat? What is your favorite main dish?

READ MARK 1:1-8.

John the Baptist told the crowds who came out to hear him preach, "One who is more powerful than I am is coming after me" (v. 7). People knew that John the Baptist was a prophet sent from God. However, it must have been stunning to hear John say, "I am not worthy to stoop down and untie the strap of his sandals" (v. 7). John was just the "undercard" or "appetizer" to get people ready for the most important one of all—Jesus Christ!

Sometimes, we can be guilty of thinking that the things of God are more important than God Himself. You must realize that no activity or pursuit, even church attendance, can take the place of Jesus.

Why do we settle for lesser important things when we know that Jesus is best?

Repentance is more than apologizing to God; it's believing that Jesus is better.

Make a list of at least three reasons why Jesus is truly better than anything the world has to offer.

1.   2.   3.

Every single day, there will be things and people trying to take the role as the main event, or main course, in your life. That is why it is so important for your heart and mind to stay focused on the truth that Jesus is better.

PRAYER MOVEMENTS

HANDS UP
A sign of surrender.

- **Read Philippians 4:6.**

Instead of worrying, go to God with thanksgiving. By faith, attune your heart and mind to who He is today. **Surrender** to the truth that He wants you to come to Him with your requests.

HANDS OPEN
A sign of emptying out.

- **Read Matthew 6:24.**

What do you need to repent of today? It may not be money, but the principle still holds true. You can't serve God and other things at the same time. **Empty out** by walking in repentance.

HANDS OUT
A sign of receiving.

- **Read John 14:1.**

Ask the Spirit to help you believe in the goodness of Jesus today. **Receive** the truth that Jesus is truly better than any distraction the world can throw at you today.

REPENTANCE IS SEEING SIN THE WAY GOD DOES

When it comes to how people view sin, the default responses are to either justify our actions or blame others. Think about it: have you ever noticed that when others sin, we tend to judge; but when we sin, we explain it away? Humans are experts at holding themselves to different standards than those they hold others to, even blaming others for their own actions.

When you make a mistake, do you tend to justify your actions or blame someone else? Why do you think you react this way?

The mark of genuine repentance and spiritual maturity is when you stop justifying your actions or blaming others and start seeing your sin the way God does.

How does God view sin?

As a follower of Jesus, the Holy Spirit will start shaping your heart and mind to view things the way your heavenly Father does. This means you'll start feeling and thinking about sin in a proper view. You can see that shift in how King David talks about his sinful actions in Psalm 51.

READ PSALM 51:1-4.

In Psalm 51:1-4, what does David say about his sin? What does he say about God?

Repentance is more than apologizing to God; it's seeing sin the way that He does.

The more you get to know Jesus, the more you'll fall in love with Him. The more you love Him, the more you'll start to hate sin. Sometimes, our greatest problem is that we still love our sin too much to walk in repentance.

Be honest. At this point in your walk with Jesus, do you tend to love your sin more than you hate it? Why do you feel this way?

David acknowledged that ultimately his sinful actions were against the Lord. Spending time with Jesus in the Scriptures and talking to Him through prayer will help you see sin the way He does. Time with the Lord will grow your love for Him.

PRAYER MOVEMENTS

HANDS OPEN
A sign of emptying out.

- **Read Luke 6:46.**

If you're going to call Jesus Lord, you need to do what He says. **Empty out** by confessing anything that is not in line with obeying Him today.

HANDS UP
A sign of surrender.

- **Read 2 Peter 3:9.**

Spend time reflecting on how patient God is and also telling Him how great He is. Voicing these truths will help remind you to **surrender** daily to who He is and know that He is worth following.

HANDS OUT
A sign of receiving.

- **Read Luke 6:40.**

A disciple follows his or her teacher closely. **Receive** any instruction that He gives you today. Daily obeying Him will shape you to be more like Him.

REPENTANCE IS PROCLAIMING JESUS TO OTHERS

READ ACTS 8:26-40.

When the gospel becomes a reality in your life, part of living a lifestyle of repentance is proclaiming Jesus to others who don't know Him. You have witnessed the beauty of forgiveness through repentance personally. Now, you get to be a witness to others, so they'll prayerfully repent and believe as well.

How would you explain the gospel to someone else?

Fear is often one of the main reasons people don't share the gospel with unbelievers. Not knowing what to say is typically one of the greatest causes of that fear.

Why is it difficult to share the gospel with others?

Here are three things you need to consider and work on in order to help dissipate fear in witnessing to your spiritually lost friends and family:

1. **Have faith in the truth of the gospel.** Do you believe it to be true?
2. **Practice explaining the gospel.** If you're basing your whole eternity on the truth of the gospel, then you should be able to explain it to others.
3. **Build confidence in sharing the gospel.** The only way to build confidence is through repetition. It may feel awkward at first, but practice sharing the gospel out loud. The more you hear yourself, the more confident you will become. The more confident you are in what you're saying, the more likely you are to share it.

How can you get practice sharing the gospel with others?

Repentance is more than apologizing to God; it's proclaiming Jesus to others.

As followers of Jesus, we should want more people to know Him, to experience the same forgiveness we have, and to live a lifestyle of repentance. That is where victory, hope, and a revival are.

PRAYER MOVEMENTS

HANDS UP
A sign of surrender.

- **Read Hebrews 12:1-2.**

Take a moment and look to Jesus. He is the perfecter of your faith. **Surrender** to the truth of who He is today and the power of the gospel. Pray for someone else who needs this truth.

HANDS OPEN
A sign of emptying out.

- **Read Luke 5:31-32.**

Is there any area of your life where you're depending on your own power? **Empty out** by trusting in the power of the Lord who is your salvation. Jesus came for people who needed Him. Pray for someone else who needs this truth.

HANDS OUT
A sign of receiving.

- **Read Romans 8:1.**

Remember, because of the gospel, there is now no condemnation for you. Take time to thank Jesus for saving you. **Receive** truth that your identity is in Jesus and never lose that hope. Pray for a friend who needs this truth.

[REPENTANCE IS LIVING DIFFERENTLY]

READ MATTHEW 5:21-48.

Jesus calls for His followers to act totally different from the rest of the world. He calls us to act in ways that contradict the natural tendencies of our human nature.

> **Why is it so difficult to love your neighbor and so easy to hate your enemy?**

Look at His revolutionary ideas about living differently:

- **Be the one to initiate reconciling a broken relationship** (vv. 21-26).
- **Intentionally avoid all sinful situations** (vv. 27-30).
- **Do not go back on your word.** If you make a commitment, keep it (vv. 33-37).
- **Go above and beyond what people expect from you.** Don't settle for mediocrity when helping others (vv. 38-42).
- **Love your enemies.** Do good to those who persecute you and pray for those who intentionally hurt you (vv. 43-48).

> **Which of these is the hardest for you to live out?**

Jesus asks us to live completely opposite to that which is normal or comfortable for us.

> **Does your lifestyle look any different from your spiritually lost friends or family members? If so, list some examples where you see a difference. If not, do you think this is okay? What needs to change?**

This is undoubtedly a very difficult lifestyle that Jesus is calling us to, but it is exactly what will attract the attention of a lost world. It's time to put these truths into practice. This is what a movement of God looks like.

Repentance is more than apologizing to God; it's living differently.

Live in a way that lets others see something different in you. When they ask you about it, that is the Holy Spirit opening a door to point them to Jesus.

PRAYER MOVEMENTS

HANDS UP
A sign of surrender.

- **Read Acts 5:31.**

Living differently is seeking Jesus above all at all times. Spend time praying and ask Him to give you the daily perspective that He sits on the throne today, alive as King of kings. **Surrender** to the truth of the forgiveness Jesus has given you.

HANDS OPEN
A sign of emptying out.

- **Read Philippians 2:4.**

Part of living differently is to serve and love others, instead of only caring about yourself. **Empty out** any selfish motives and attitudes today. A real movement of God will propel us to love and care for others as well.

HANDS OUT
A sign of receiving.

- **Read Romans 2:4.**

Ask God to remind you of His kindness today. God has called you to live a lifestyle of receiving His kindness but also extending it toward others. Don't despise His kindness; **receive** His kindness. His kindness leads us to repentance.

SESSION 4:
FAITH

IT'S MORE THAN BELIEVING GOD EXISTS

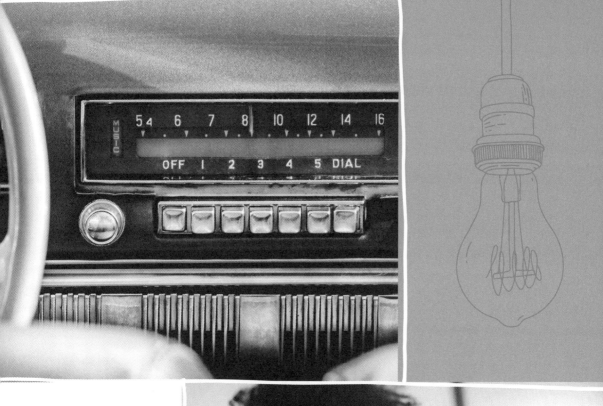

Video Guide

KEY SCRIPTURE: Acts 5:40-42

1. Faith is _____ than just believing God exists.

> "Even the demons believe—and tremble!"
> JAMES 2:19 (NKJV)

2. Revival is _____ to how big God is an knowing that you can fully trust Him.

3. Big faith will lead to big _____.

> "For me, to live is Christ and to die is gain."
> PHILIPPIANS 1:21

4. Do you just believe God exists, or do you truly have _____ in Him?

Group Time

What's the difference between believing God exists and having faith in God?

Is it enough to just believe that God exists? Why or why not?

GOOD COMPANY? Just believing God exists doesn't put you in very good company. Don't believe me? Take a look at James 2:19.

> "You believe that God is one. Good! Even the demons believe—and they shudder." **JAMES 2:19**

When we look at the world and all the bad things that happen every day, it can sometimes be difficult to have faith. Many people (maybe, even you) are asking the question, "Where is God?"

Spiritual awakening occurs when we don't fully understand everything that is going on around us, and we still trust Him.

The word **FAITH** is rooted in the Greek word *pistis* or *pistueo*, which means "trust, belief, confidence, and assurance." We have faith in the Lord when we fully trust that He is working, even when we can't see Him or understand what He is doing.

Why is it sometimes easier to believe that God exists than it is to actually trust Him with your life?

What is one area of your life that you have a difficult time trusting Jesus with?

Revival happens when the Spirit awakens you to how big He really is, so that you will have a big faith in a big God.

BELIEVE IT & LIVE IT

READ ACTS 5:27-42.

²⁷ After they brought them in, they had them stand before the Sanhedrin, and the high priest asked, ²⁸ "Didn't we strictly order you not to teach in this name? Look, you have filled Jerusalem with your teaching and are determined to make us guilty of this man's blood." ²⁹ Peter and the apostles replied, "We must obey God rather than people. ³⁰ The God of our ancestors raised up Jesus, whom you had murdered by hanging him on a tree. ³¹ God exalted this man to his right hand as ruler and Savior, to give repentance to Israel and forgiveness of sins. ³² We are witnesses of these things, and so is the Holy Spirit whom God has given to those who obey him." ³³ When they heard this, they were enraged and wanted to kill them. ³⁴ But a Pharisee named Gamaliel, a teacher of the law who was respected by all the people, stood up in the Sanhedrin and ordered the men to be taken outside for a little while. ³⁵ He said to them, "Men of Israel, be careful about what you're about to do to these men. ³⁶ Some time ago Theudas rose up, claiming to be somebody, and a group of about four hundred men rallied to him. He was killed, and all his followers were dispersed and came to nothing. ³⁷ After this man, Judas the Galilean rose up in the days of the census and attracted a following. He also perished, and all his followers were scattered. ³⁸ So in the present case, I tell you, stay away from these men and leave them alone. For if this plan or this work is of human origin, it will fail; ³⁹ but if it is of God, you will not be able to overthrow them. You may even be found fighting against God." They were persuaded by him. ⁴⁰ After they called in the apostles and had them flogged, they ordered them not to speak in the name of Jesus and released them. ⁴¹ Then they went out from the presence of the Sanhedrin, rejoicing that they were counted worthy to be treated shamefully on behalf of the Name. ⁴² Every day in the temple, and in various homes, they continued teaching and proclaiming the good news that Jesus is the Messiah. **ACTS 5:27-42**

This has become one of my favorite stories in the Bible because of the boldness and fearlessness of the disciples, even in the face of these religious leaders who were acting like bullies. Through faith in Christ and the power of the Holy Spirit, the disciples had been spreading the name of the Lord Jesus all across Jerusalem. Because of this, they were brought before the Sanhedrin, a legislative council made up of religious leaders called Pharisees, Sadducees, and scribes. These people often fought and argued with each other, but one thing they agreed upon was how much they hated Jesus and disliked His followers.

Why do some (even religious people) have a difficult time trusting in Jesus?

Why would religious people hate Jesus?

In spite of verbal threats and actual physical persecution, the disciples were not deterred from their mission of sharing the gospel. Why are they so bold and fearless? Because of their unrelenting faith in who Jesus is and their identity in Christ as His followers. They had nothing to fear, and they lived like it. Faith is more than believing God exists, it's actually trusting God with your life.

List three or more ways the disciples showed their faith in Acts 5:27-42.

Even in the face of so much opposition, what was the driving motivation for the disciples to be so bold?

"We must obey God rather than people." **ACTS 5:29**

When personal revival happens in your life, it will refocus your faith in Jesus so much that it will propel you toward full obedience to God. Sadly, when we're not fully trusting in Jesus, we tend to be more concerned about being people pleasers than God pleasers, being more politically correct than biblically correct, and being more popular than holy. However, if you want to truly be relevant, then stick to faith in Jesus and stick to obedience. You really have nothing to fear.

Why is it sometimes easier to be motivated to obey people instead of God?

HOW DO WE WALK IN FAITH INSTEAD OF FEAR?

In Acts 5:34-39, a Pharisee named Gamaliel presented a very reasonable case and made an appeal to the rest of the council. He gave a couple of examples of previous leaders whose followers scattered as soon as those leaders died. Then, Gamaliel (who was not a Christian) made a statement that has remained true for two thousand years.

[38] "For if this plan or this work is of human origin, it will fail; [39] but if it is of God, you will not be able to overthrow them. You may even be found fighting against God." **ACTS 5:38-39**

Movements that are started and powered by humans will eventually fail. However, movements that are started and powered by God cannot be stopped.

What is something humans have started that eventually failed?

Does it give you confidence knowing that you are part of a movement of God that can't be stopped? How does this change the way you live?

The disciples knew that they were a part of a movement of God that could not be overthrown. They were full of faith, so they had no room for fear.

Is your day-to-day life marked more by faith or fear? Why?

The disciples would eventually be beaten and charged to stop talking about Jesus. However, after they were released, they immediately started rejoicing that they were counted worthy to be treated shamefully for Jesus. Then, they went and told everyone they could about Him.

How do you stop disciples who are fearless, full of faith, and know they're a part of a movement that can't be stopped? The answer is: YOU CAN'T! If you beat them, they rejoice. If you tell them to shut up about Jesus, they tell everyone about Him. If you kill them, then they get to go be with Jesus. Ultimately, because of their faith, you can't stop them from obeying God instead of humans.

> "Got any rivers you think are uncrossable?
> Got any mountains you can't tunnel through?
> God specializes in things thought impossible. And
> He can do what no other power can do."[1]
>
> LEONARD RAVENHILL

These disciples realized that they had the all-powerful, nothing-is-impossible God living inside of them, and they were a part of a movement that could not be stopped. And that made them absolutely fearless.

What do you need to start having faith in God about right now?

How is trusting God with this going to help you start obeying Him?

When have you seen the power of God in your life? How can placing your unflinching trust in His power change your life today?

FAITH IS TRUSTING THAT GOD HAS REVEALED HIMSELF

READ JOHN 1:14-18.

Have you ever thought to yourself, *If God is real, then why doesn't He just reveal Himself? Why won't He just speak to us in a loud audible voice saying, "Hey, here I am! This is what I'm like"?* If God would just let us all see Him, then surely everyone would believe. After all, it's really difficult for people to believe in Someone they can't see or touch. Right?

Why is it difficult to believe that God is real?

Guess what? That is exactly what God did! He showed Himself and spoke to us through Jesus Christ.

John 1 presents to us a beautiful idea of who Jesus is. God went on a mission trip to planet earth. "The Word became flesh and dwelt among us. We observed his glory, the glory as the one and only Son from the Father, full of grace and truth" (v. 14). Jesus is the perfect representation of what God the Father is really like. God revealed Himself to His creation, and many still did not believe. In fact, they crucified Him!

List three or more characteristics you see in Jesus in the Bible:

Want to know what God is like? Look to Jesus. Anything you see in Jesus is actually God choosing to reveal Himself because Jesus is God.

Faith is more than believing God exists; it's trusting that God has revealed Himself.

"No one has ever seen God. The one and only Son, who is himself God and is at the Father's side—he has revealed him" (v. 18). Realize today that you serve a God who loves you so much that He took the time to reveal Himself to you through His only Son, Jesus Christ. Jesus Himself said, "The one who has seen me has seen the Father" (John 14:9). Let God reveal Himself to you today through the Scriptures and by talking to Him in prayer.

PRAYER MOVEMENTS

HANDS UP
A sign of surrender.

- **Read Romans 15:13.**

Spend time reflecting on how God has revealed Himself. Tell Him what you love about Him. **Surrender** any unbelief to Him, and let Him replace it with joy and peace.

HANDS OPEN
A sign of emptying out.

- **Read Philippians 4:8.**

What are you focusing on right now that is not true, honorable, just, pure, lovely, or commendable? **Empty out** by confessing anything that is not in line with who He is. Dwell on the beauty of Jesus today.

HANDS OUT
A sign of receiving.

- **Read 1 Timothy 6:11.**

A follower of Jesus flees from unrighteous things and walks in righteous things. **Receive** the call to pursue good things today through the power of the Holy Spirit. If you pursue Jesus, you will pursue the right things.

[FAITH IS TRUSTING HIM EVEN WHEN YOU DON'T UNDERSTAND EVERYTHING]

READ PROVERBS 3:5-6.

If you could ask God anything, what would it be?

It's extremely easy to be confused about what faith is. Often, people will try to approach God with this logic: *God, once I fully understand everything, then I will trust You. Then, and only then, will I believe in You.* However, we don't approach other things in our lives like that. Every day, we place our faith in things that we don't fully understand.

What are some things that you place your trust in every day but don't fully understand how they work?

Faith is not, *God, once I fully understand, then I will trust You.* Faith is, *God, I don't understand everything about You, and I don't fully understand what You're doing. But I trust You.* The truth is it isn't even possible to fully understand everything there is to know about God.

What is something about God that you wish you could understand more?

Think about it, if our human minds could fully understand everything there is to know about God, then He wouldn't be God. That would make Him equal, or even less than us. In fact, the only things that our finite minds can truly understand about the infinite mind of God is what He chooses to reveal to us.

King Solomon, the writer of some of the Proverbs, said in Proverbs 3:5-6 that you must trust in the Lord and not rely on your own understanding. He will lead you through paths that He has made straight, but you have to know Him by faith.

Faith is more than believing God exists; it's trusting Him even when you don't understand everything.

Even though you'll never fully understand everything there is to know about God, you can and should still grow in your wisdom and faith. That is why it is so important to stay in the Bible and spend time with God in prayer.

PRAYER MOVEMENTS

HANDS OPEN
A sign of emptying out.

- **Read Mark 9:24.**

In what areas of your life are you not trusting the Lord? **Empty out** by confessing unbelief and ask the Lord to replace unbelief with faith.

HANDS UP
A sign of surrender.

- **Read Hebrews 11:1.**

Surrender today to the truth of who God is. By faith, trust Him. Pray and ask God to strengthen your faith, even when you can't see Him.

HANDS OUT
A sign of receiving.

- **Read 2 Corinthians 5:7.**

Ask the Spirit to help you believe in the goodness of Jesus today. **Receive** the truth that Jesus can be trusted even when you can't see Him. Walk in that truth today.

FAITH IS TRUSTING GOD WITH EVERY AREA OF YOUR LIFE

READ COLOSSIANS 1:17-18.

When people visit our houses, we want to be a good host. So, we'll say, "Make yourself at home." However, when we say that to someone, we don't really mean it. How weird would it be if that person started looking around your room and going through you stuff?

What rooms or areas of your house are off-limits to guests?

When we say, "Make yourself at home," we don't want people to act like they really own the place. Sadly, many people approach Jesus the same way. What we really mean is, "Jesus, You can hang out in my Sunday morning room, but stay out of my relationships room, my school room, and my phone room." However, you need to know that when Jesus comes into your life, He buys the whole house and now has access to every area.

What areas of your life are closed off to Jesus?

Whatever they are, it's time to open them up to Him. For Jesus to truly have "first place in everything" (v. 18), He has to have access to do whatever He wants.

Do you really trust that He can do a better job with those areas of your life than you can? Why or why not?

There's an old cliché that still holds true. If Jesus isn't Lord over all in your life, then He is not Lord at all in your life. Here is the reality: you and Jesus don't rule together. He is King. He is Lord. He is God. You are not.

Faith is more than believing God exists; it's trusting God with every area of your life.

As a follower of Jesus, you can trust that He is better at owning the house, cleaning the house, and ruling the house than you are. When He is first place in every area of your life, that is when you'll have victory, freedom, and revival.

PRAYER MOVEMENTS

HANDS UP
A sign of surrender.

- **Read Romans 5:1.**

Take a moment and reflect on what Jesus did to buy your house (life). **Surrender** to the truth that He is the One in charge. He rules the house. He is your King and Lord.

HANDS OPEN
A sign of emptying out.

- **Read Romans 12:3.**

Typically, trying to be in charge of your own life and controlling certain areas is a pride problem. **Empty out** by confessing the areas of your life that you've tried to control. Ask God to give you faith to trust Him with those areas.

HANDS OUT
A sign of receiving.

- **Read Romans 8:1.**

Remember, if you've been bought by the blood of Jesus and His Spirit lives in you, you are now a child of the most high God. Take time to thank Jesus for purchasing you. **Receive** that truth today and live under His control knowing that He is doing all things for His glory and your good.

FAITH IS TRUSTING GOD EVEN WHEN YOU'RE FACING TEMPTATION

READ LUKE 4:1-4,13.

One of the smartest marketing schemes that I have ever fallen victim to was at an amusement park. While waiting in a two-hour line for a popular roller coaster in one hundred degree heat, I came face-to-face with what I needed most: a huge trough full of ice-cold bottled water. Needless to say, I gave in to the temptation and bought one of the most expensive bottles of water I've ever paid for.

What is something that you paid a ridiculous amount of money for because you had to have it in that very moment?

Jesus had been in the hot, dry, and treacherous desert for forty days without food. It was only fitting for Satan to tempt Him to turn stones into bread. However, Jesus refused to give in. He knew His obligation to please the Father was more important than pleasing His flesh.

What are some of the things that people your age are tempted with the most?

Satan knows our weaknesses, so it only makes sense for him to tempt us with the things we desire. If you struggle with lust, Satan probably isn't going to lure you with gossip. If you struggle with gossiping, he is not going to waste his time tempting you with alcohol.

What is something the enemy tends to tempt you with?

Faith is more than believing God exists; it's trusting God even when you're facing temptation.

Know your weaknesses and be ready to combat Satan in those areas before he ever tempts you. Even when the temptation comes, remember that God is faithful to offer a way of escape.

PRAYER MOVEMENTS

HANDS OPEN
A sign of emptying out.

• **Read James 1:13.**

Realize today that God never tempts you. **Empty out** by confessing the things that you are tempted by. A real movement of God propels us towards obedience.

HANDS UP
A sign of surrender.

• **Read John 6:29.**

Spend time praying to God and confess your continued belief in the Son of God. **Surrender** to the truth that Jesus is better than anything you can be tempted by.

HANDS OUT
A sign of receiving.

• **Read 1 Corinthians 10:13.**

Ask God to remind you of His faithfulness today. God has called you to live a lifestyle of obedience and holiness through His power. **Receive** the promise of a way out of temptation when God provides it, and ask Him to give you the faith to walk through that way of escape.

SESSION 5:
OBEDIENCE

IT'S MORE THAN A "GET OUT OF HELL FREE" CARD

Video Guide

KEY SCRIPTURE: Isaiah 6:1-9

1. Obedience is more than a "get out of hell free" _____.

2. The gospel saves us to a relationship with God, to the family of God, to a mission, and to _____.

3. Earthly kings die, but there's a King of all kings who always _____.

4. When you come face to face with the greatness of who the King is, _____ comes to the surface.

5. The moment you say yes to Jesus at salvation, yes is the _____ answer you can ever give Him again.

6. God saves us to _____ us.

Group Time

Why is it sometimes difficult to obey God?

When has God called you to do something, but, for whatever reason, you disobeyed Him?

WHO WAS ANNIE? Annie Armstrong was born in Baltimore on July 11, 1850.[1] She became a follower of Jesus at twenty years old, and through the Lord working in her heart, she became passionate about missions, serving the poor, and social justice. There weren't a lot of opportunities at that time for women to create, serve, or lead. However, she did not let those roadblocks deter her from obeying what she believed the Lord was calling her to do.

In 1888, Annie was a key part of forming the Woman's Missionary Union (WMU).[2] Much like today, missionaries desperately needed support and resources. Annie helped mobilize women from all over the nation to help educate local churches on biblical missions. She raised funds for missionaries and heightened the involvement of believers in the mission of God. Her passion and obedience to the Lord could best be described as zealous. In fact, she reported that "in a ten-year span she had written 77,447 letters and manuscripts."[3]

In 1934, a Special Easter Offering for Home Missions was named in her honor.[4] Today, tens of thousands of churches give a special financial gift every year known as the Annie Armstrong Easter Offering. The obedience of Christians giving to this offering generates millions of dollars annually to support missionaries, church planters, and the advancement of the gospel all across North America. Ultimately, it helps millions of people hear about Jesus.[5]

This all started with one young lady obeying the call of God on her life. Through her obedience and the power of the Holy Spirit, she helped many other believers walk in obedience and advance the kingdom of God. We still feel the impact of her obedience well over a hundred years later.

What is something you believe God is calling you to today?

Is it something God is calling for your obedience to do, but you're fearful of the push back that you could possibly receive from others? How do you overcome that fear?

OBEDIENCE is hearing the calling of God on your life and acting on it.

Often, the kingdom of God is expanded by one small step of obedience at a time. In following Jesus, our success is not in massive results (that's up to Him); it's in small acts of obedience.

A movement of God happens when the people of God start living in full obedience to their God.

BELIEVE IT & LIVE IT

READ ISAIAH 6:1-8.

¹ In the year that King Uzziah died, I saw the Lord seated on a high and lofty throne, and the hem of his robe filled the temple. ² Seraphim were standing above him; they each had six wings: with two they covered their faces, with two they covered their feet, and with two they flew. ³ And one called to another: Holy, holy, holy is the Lᴏʀᴅ of Armies; his glory fills the whole earth. ⁴ The foundations of the doorways shook at the sound of their voices, and the temple was filled with smoke. ⁵ Then I said: Woe is me for I am ruined because I am a man of unclean lips and live among a people of unclean lips, and because my eyes have seen the King, the Lᴏʀᴅ of Armies. ⁶ Then one of the seraphim flew to me, and in his hand was a glowing coal that he had taken from the altar with tongs. ⁷ He touched my mouth with it and said: Now that this has touched your lips, your iniquity is removed and your sin is atoned for. ⁸ Then I heard the voice of the Lord asking: Who will I send? Who will go for us? I said: Here I am. Send me. **ISAIAH 6:1-8**

Isaiah lived about 700 years before the birth of Christ. Isaiah 6 shares the story of his calling to obedience. Personally, I love that Isaiah began by pointing out that in the same year that an earthly king died, he saw another King very much alive. Many Bible scholars believe that Isaiah is describing the preincarnate Christ.

Preincarnate Christ: The Son of God (who is eternal) revealing Himself throughout the Old Testament before the birth of Jesus in Bethlehem.

> How does it make you feel knowing that Jesus is a King who has lived forever?

In Isaiah's vision, he described seeing seraphim, or angels (v. 2), worshiping the Lord. They sing over and over that He is holy (v. 3), which means "He is set apart." Basically, there is no one else like this King. He really is the King of all kings.

Kings carry an authority that requires allegiance and obedience in their kingdoms. In fact, there are really only three types of people in every kingdom: the King, subjects who obey the king, and people who live in disobedience and rebellion against the king.

> Since you're not the King (Jesus), how can you tell which type of citizen of His kingdom you are?

Then, in verse 5, Isaiah was confronted with his own sin. Being in the presence of the holiness of the Lord will draw our sin to the surface. Isaiah confessed his sin, and the King atoned for it (vv. 6-7).

> Have you ever wondered how people were "saved" in the Old Testament? How would you explain it?

Steven Lawson says it like this, "In the Old Testament, they were saved by grace alone, through faith alone, in Christ alone, looking ahead to the coming of Christ."[6] Today, by faith and repentance, we look back at the coming of Christ, His crucifixion, and resurrection and believe. The Old Testament believers looked forward to the same things and by faith and repentance believed.

As an illustration, it could compared to the way a credit card works—you get the goods now, but it's paid for later. Isaiah's sin was now forgiven and atoned for by the King. That very same King would pay for it later with His life, death on the cross, and eventual resurrection. This is Isaiah's testimony of salvation.

> Take a moment and on another piece of paper, write out your testimony. What were you like before you met Jesus? How did you meet Jesus? What is your life like now that you know Him?

WHAT IS GOD CALLING YOU TO SAY YES TO?

When the King saves us from our sin, it does not work like a Monopoly "get out of hell free" card. If you've ever played the board game, you know it's possible to land on the Chance or Community Chest spots and draw the Get Out of Jail Free card to hold on to just in case you go to jail. You put that card in your stack and forget all about it, until you need it. Sadly, many people think gospel the works like this, too.

However, salvation is not the card you play when you die and stand before God. Salvation and the eternal life it promises change your life now. It's about obedience now. The gospel doesn't just save us *from* things—hell, death, sin, and destruction—it also calls us *to* things (to a relationship with the King, a mission, a purpose in life, and obedience). Following Jesus is all about obeying Him.

> How do we change our mindset that salvation is not just our "get out of hell" card but the purpose of our lives today?

Isaiah 6:8 is one of the most famous verses of the Bible. You've probably seen it on the back of a missions t-shirt before: "Then I heard the voice of the Lord asking: Who will I send? Who will go for us? I said: Here I am. Send me." The King saves us to send us. The King called Isaiah to go to the people around Him, and he responded in obedience with, "YES!"

As a follower of Jesus, saying, "No, Lord. No, King," does not work. The moment you said yes to Jesus at salvation, yes became the only answer you can ever give Him again.

"We should not pray for revival unless we are ready to be turned upside down, our heads and our pockets and our lives shaken out."[7]

GREG LAURIE

Where is the King sending you to tell people about Him?

When God's people live a life of complete obedience, revival can be felt because schools, communities, and nations will be affected. The King has done the work to save you. Now, He is calling you to be sent and is asking if you are willing to go. Are you willing to obey and say yes?

OBEDIENCE IS OBEYING GOD EVEN WHEN IT'S DIFFICULT

READ ISAIAH 6:9-13.

When Isaiah 6 is taught, people often stop with verse 8. Then, with excitement, ask something like, "God is calling you, will you obey? Let's go! He is sending us." Of course, all of that is true and vital—God saves us to send us. However, Isaiah 6 doesn't stop at verse 8.

In verses 9-13, you'll see that the King sent Isaiah to point people to God. However, it was not going to be easy. The reality is that being obedient to the Lord is often not going to be received well by the world around us.

What makes obeying a calling like this difficult?

Have you ever experienced push back or minor persecution because you were obeying the Lord? What happened?

Remember, Jesus does not promise us an easy life. He promises us an eternal life. Obeying the Lord will often make living in the world more difficult. However, we will be more joyful, fulfilled, and at peace because we are being obedient to our great King.

In verse 13, the King sent Isaiah out to be faithful to the "stump." What this means is that no matter how bad the world gets, there will always be people who faithfully obey the Lord. For Isaiah, this stump would eventually turn into a flourishing tree with many people now in the kingdom of God.

Obedience is more than a "get out of hell free" card; it's obeying God even when it's difficult.

Ultimately, this challenging environment was Isaiah's ministry. God was sending him, and Isaiah obeyed.

Where is God sending you?

Are you willing to say yes, even when it's going to be difficult?

PRAYER MOVEMENTS

HANDS OPEN
A sign of emptying out.

- **Read Acts 13:47.**

Are you willing to be sent out to point people to the King? **Empty out** by confessing any fears and hesitations you have. Ask God to replace fear with confidence.

HANDS UP
A sign of surrender.

- **Read Acts 1:8.**

Spend time reflecting on how the Holy Spirit is with you in power. Tell Him how you need His presence while you're in your daily mission field. **Surrender** to His calling.

HANDS OUT
A sign of receiving.

- **Read Mark 16:15.**

God's plan in reaching the world with the gospel is the church. There is no back-up plan. **Receive** the call to *go*. This call isn't for a few super-Christians; it's for all Christians. Pray for your mission field today.

OBEDIENCE IS A LIFESTYLE CHANGE RIGHT NOW

READ MARK 1:16-20.

What is your favorite hobby?

In Mark 1, Jesus called Peter, Andrew, James, and John to drop their nets and follow Him. For them, fishing was way more than a hobby; it was their job.

What is your dream job?

Notice they didn't say to Jesus, "Thanks, but we'll just catch You the next time You come through town," or, "Hey, we'll follow You and listen to what You have to say, but don't ask us to do anything." In fact, by dropping their nets—truly, walking away from their careers—they were saying the exact opposite.

Would it be difficult or scary for your life or plans to be completely changed by Jesus? Why?

Over time, these disciples would be taught by Jesus and would put His teaching into practice by fishing for people. They didn't always get it right, nor did they always fully understand what Jesus was asking them to do. However, they were on a journey of following and obeying Jesus, and once they received the Holy Spirit (see Acts 2), they grew tremendously. They went all in with their faith, and God would turn the world upside down through these ordinary men who decided to follow and obey an extraordinary Jesus.

Before being used to reach people with the message of Jesus, their first step was to drop their nets in obedience. They had to leave behind their past, their comforts, and anything that would distract them from the primary call on their lives—to know Jesus and to make Him known.

Obedience is more than a "get out of hell free" card; it's a lifestyle change right now.

As a follower of Jesus, you can trust that He is a lot better at directing how you should live this life than you are. When you obey Him with your life, that is when you'll truly be fulfilled because you're living with real purpose. Often, His plan for your life will look completely different than your own, but His plan is always better.

PRAYER MOVEMENTS

 **HANDS UP**
A sign of surrender.

- **Read Exodus 34:6.**

Take a moment and reflect on who the unchanging God really is. **Surrender** to the truth that who He was in Exodus 34 is who He still is today. He can be trusted; therefore, He should be obeyed.

 **HANDS OPEN**
A sign of emptying out.

- **Read John 14:15.**

It's easy to say you love Jesus, but it takes faith and obedience to show your love for Him. **Empty out** by confessing the areas of your life you don't trust or obey Jesus with. Ask God to continue to grow your love for Him. When you love Him, you'll desire to obey Him.

 **HANDS OUT**
A sign of receiving.

- **Read Hebrews 13:16.**

Remember, the sacrifices the Lord wants from us are to obey Him by doing what is good through the power of His Spirit and to share Him with others. **Receive** that truth today and live by walking in obedience to whatever He is calling you to.

OBEDIENCE IS BEING THE CHURCH TODAY

READ 2 CORINTHIANS 5:17-19.

What does it mean to be a new creation?

As a student, you'll often hear people say that you are the future of the church. I've even been guilty of saying this, too. What they mean is you are the future leaders and influencers of the church. However, according to the New Testament, if you've been bought by the blood of Jesus and the Holy Spirit of God lives inside of you, **you are the church right now!** You have purpose now. You have a calling on your life now. You are called to ministry right now.

What does it mean to be the church?

How does realizing that you are the church now change your perspective?

So, in light of the King sending you into your daily mission field, who is He calling you to share the gospel with? Not only has He given you a ministry of reconciliation (v. 18), He has also given you a message of reconciliation (v. 19)—the gospel.

Who is one person that you can begin to pray for every day asking God to save them, to open their heart to the gospel, and to provide you an opportunity to share the good news of Jesus with them?

I'm asked all the time what the "secret sauce" is to reaching your generation. You know better than I do that there is no secret sauce, but there is a powerful, life-changing gospel. And that is what all generations desperately need.

Obedience is more than a "get out of hell free" card; it's being the church today.

One of the goals of this Bible study is to cultivate your heart to go tell people about Jesus by helping you spend time with the Lord in Scripture reading and in prayer every day. Personally, when I am walking in intimacy with God, then I will naturally share out of the overflow of my own worship of Jesus.

PRAYER MOVEMENTS

HANDS OPEN
A sign of emptying out.

- **Read Matthew 28:19.**

What hesitations do you have today about being sent by the King to *go*? **Empty out** by confessing fear and complacency. Ask the Lord to replace them with obedience and passion for people who don't know Jesus.

HANDS UP
A sign of surrender.

- **Read Matthew 28:18.**

Surrender today to the truth of the authority of who Jesus is. By obedience, trust Him as King. Pray and ask the King to show you at least one person in your life who does not know Him.

HANDS OUT
A sign of receiving.

- **Read Matthew 28:20.**

Ask the Spirit to help you trust and obey His presence in you. **Receive** the calling on your life to go where He is sending you to make Him known. Walk in that obedience today.

OBEDIENCE IS LIVING ON MISSION OUTSIDE THE WALLS OF A CHURCH BUILDING

READ MATTHEW 5:13-16.

There are many Christians who believe that they are to separate themselves from the world completely. They feel that the more they hide themselves, the more spiritual they become. Sadly, many churches have come to adopt this same mentality. They want their group of people just like them in the church, and they don't want anyone coming in who is different. Many churches have become a private little club for insiders only.

On a scale of 1 to 10 (10 being the best), how do you feel your church or student ministry does at reaching and accepting new people?

Why did you give your church or student ministry this score?

Jesus implored His followers to be salt and light (vv. 13-14). Salt preserved food when there was no such thing as refrigerators or freezers. God has called us to preserve culture by pointing people to the gospel. Light breaks darkness and attracts those who are in need of seeing. Jesus told His listeners not to hide their light. We need followers of Christ who are not scared to have God shine through them so brightly that they affect the world around them.

Obedience is more than a "get out of hell free" card; it's living on mission outside the walls of a church building.

Someone once said that for salt to be used properly, you have to get it out of the saltshaker. It's good for the church to gather together to worship, to hear the teaching of the Scriptures, to be discipled, and to encourage one another. However, for the church to truly be obedient, it has to leave the building and influence the world around it.

What are some practical ways that you can allow God to shine through you this week, so that you can point people to the Light of the world?

PRAYER MOVEMENTS

HANDS UP
A sign of surrender.

- **Psalm 47:2.**

Spend time praying to the Lord and being reminded of how awesome He is. **Surrender** to the truth that He is a great King over the whole earth. It all belongs to Him.

HANDS OPEN
A sign of emptying out.

- **Read Acts 26:16.**

Realize today that God is calling you to obey Him and make Him known in your daily mission fields. **Empty out** by confessing the things that are keeping you from walking in this obedience. A real movement of God will propel us toward obedience and to influence others.

HANDS OUT
A sign of receiving.

- **Read Luke 10:27.**

God has called you to love Him and love others. **Receive** this truth today. How is God calling you to love Him today? The best way to love your neighbors is to tell them about Jesus.

SESSION 6:
HOLINESS

IT'S MORE
THAN A HALO

Video Guide

KEY SCRIPTURE: 1 Peter 1:15-16

1. Holiness is more than a _____. Holiness is being set apart by a holy God to live _____.

2. Holiness is being changed by a holy God to start _____ the culture around you.

3. Holiness is actually an _____ change.

4. When God changes who you _____ , He will change what you _____.

5. When your identity has changed and you are now a _____ of the most high God, don't live in your _____ anymore.

6. God has changed who you _____, and over time, the power of the Holy Spirit will change what you _____.

Group Time

RETRAIN THE DONKEYS. In the early 1900s, there was a movement of God that swept across Wales that is known today as the Welsh Revival. On September 29, 1904, a young man by the name of Evan Roberts was in a meeting with other students at Blaenannerch Chapel.[1] It was in this meeting where he sensed that God answered his prayer, and through the Spirit's power, he was filled with confidence, walked in holiness, and was passionate about reaching Wales with the gospel. Not long after this night, the sparks of revival began to turn into an inferno that spread across the nation. Evan found himself in a key role of this movement of God. However, he was neither a great organizer nor an eloquent preacher.[2]

> If you had a one sentence prayer for revival in your life, what would it be?

As revival broke out across the nation, church buildings began to fill to capacity with many people coming to faith in Christ, repenting of their sins, and desiring to live differently. Some historians have described the revival as having the furthest reaching impact compared to others of its kind—the movement spread to many other areas, such as India, Korea, China, Africa, and Latin America.[3]

Often, the truest proofs of a genuine revival is when people actually start living differently, and the fruit of the Spirit are evident (see Gal. 5). One of the key components often preached during this movement of God was repentance of sin and living in holiness through the empowerment of the Holy Spirit. J. Edwin Orr, who studied this revival extensively, said this about the country during the time of this spiritual awakening,

> *Many taverns went bankrupt. The police became unemployed in many districts, because there was no longer any crime. Stoppages occurred in coal mines, not due to unpleasantness between management and workers, but because so many foul-mouthed miners became converted and stopped using foul language that the donkeys which hauled the coal trucks in the mines could no longer understand what was being said to them.*[4]

Now that is what I call a movement of God! These coal miners, who originally trained their donkeys to use cuss words as commands, had to retrain the donkeys because those same miners began following Jesus and no longer wanted to talk that way. When a holy God captures your heart, you should have a desire to walk in holiness through the power of the Holy Spirit.

When you hear the words *holy* or *holiness,* what comes to mind?

HOLINESS is being set apart by God to live differently than the world around us.

To be clear, holiness is completely a work of God in your life. He sets you apart instantaneously by saving you through the work of the gospel, then over time, through the sanctifying work of the Holy Spirit, you should begin to live differently. It's an inside-out process; what's on the inside should start becoming evident on the outside.

A movement of God in your life doesn't mean you'll be perfect. However, the desire and power to live in holiness should be evident.

How is it possible to match an inner desire to live set apart for Jesus with the ability to actually do it?

BELIEVE IT & LIVE IT

READ 1 PETER 1:13-17.

> [13] Therefore, with your minds ready for action, be sober-minded and set your hope completely on the grace to be brought to you at the revelation of Jesus Christ. [14] As obedient children, do not be conformed to the desires of your former ignorance. [15] But as the one who called you is holy, you also are to be holy in all your conduct; [16] for it is written, Be holy, because I am holy. [17] If you appeal to the Father who judges impartially according to each one's work, you are to conduct yourselves in reverence during your time living as strangers.
> **1 PETER 1:13-17**

Peter, one of the original twelve disciples of Jesus, reminded his original audience (persecuted Christians in exile) of the truth of the gospel in their lives. The reason he reminded them of the gospel is because the gospel is the work of God in their lives that literally changed their identity. They were now "obedient children" (v. 14), and as children of the most high God, they could no longer live like they did as spiritual orphans. They had to live differently.

Christians at that time were under extreme persecution. In fact, many of them fled their cities and homes for safety. That is why they were exiles. Because of the persecution they faced, it would have been easier to go back to their old ways of doing things. Being a follower of Jesus was costing them everything.

Why is it so easy to fall back into old habits?

This is why Peter reminded them (and us) that God is holy (v. 15). There is no one like Him. He is the one true and living God. Also, if He is holy and His Spirit lives inside of us, we should be holy, too (v. 16). After all, if we are filled with the Holy Spirit, we will become a holy people that are set apart to live differently from the world around us. One Bible commentary explains it like this, "The idea of holiness for God's people includes not simply a concept of 'separation' in general but a specifically moral sense of separation from evil and a dedication to a life of righteousness."[5]

The Holy Spirit inside of you should be propelling you to be more like Christ every day. Over time your character and love should begin to look more and more like His. "Be holy yourselves in all your conduct speaks of a pattern of life that transforms every day, every moment, every thought, and every action."[6]

Does your life look any different from your spiritually lost friends or family? How so?

HOW DO WE LIVE OUT BIBLICAL HOLINESS?

Biblical holiness comes from the overflow of your identity in Christ and the power of the Holy Spirit. At salvation, you went from being:

- spiritually lost to being spiritually found.
- a sinner separated from God to a saint who is one with God.
- spiritually dead to being spiritually alive.
- empty to being filled with the Holy Spirit.
- a broken person to a new creation in Christ.
- an orphan because of sin to being a child of God because of salvation.[7]

> Take a picture of this list or write it out on a piece of paper. Then, put it somewhere you will see every day. What does this list remind you of?

You need to be reminded often of your new identity in Christ. Discipleship and sanctification is a lifelong process of learning how to live out your new identity. Moment by moment and day by day, as you grow in your relationship with Him, you learn what it means to live as a child of God, a follower of Jesus, a Christian. A Holy God inside of you is making you holy.

God changes who you **are,** but He will also change what you **do.** He addresses our **identity,** then He addresses our **activity.**

> Describe how it feels to know that you don't have to try to change by your own power because there is a greater power living in you that leads you to change.

> "Revival is the visitation of God which brings to life Christians who have been sleeping and restores a deep sense of God's near presence and holiness."[8]
>
> J. I. PACKER

When we as believers fully grasp this truth, then we will see a movement of God begin to take place in our lives. The presence of God changes who we **are** before it changes what we **do.** The Holy Spirit will change your **identity,** and over time, He will begin to change your **activity.** It truly is a journey of learning about the holiness of God—how to be who He made you to be—which will translate into holy living.

What habits need to change in your life in order to strengthen your relationship with God and grow in your new identity?

[HOLINESS IS AVOIDING LEGALISM]

When you hear the word *legalism*, what comes to mind?

Legalism is the belief that you can earn your salvation and grow in sanctification by good works purely out of your own efforts. Often, people who struggle with legalism push their preferences and stances on everyone else. To be clear, I am not talking about clear biblical commands; I'm talking about preferences. For example, a person might feel like it's wrong to watch movies on Sunday. There's nothing wrong with abstaining from watching a movie on Sunday, but if this person starts to think that everyone should not watch movies on Sunday and all those who do don't love Jesus, that's a problem. Sadly, legalism is one of the biggest contributors in driving people away from the church.

How have you experienced legalism in your life?

READ 1 PETER 1:13-16.

In these verses, Peter reveals how the gospel works in your life. God changes who you are, then He changes what you do. He addresses our identity, then He addresses our activity. Legalism tries to invert those. It guilts you into trying to be perfect and working hard by your own efforts to make sure your halo doesn't fall off.

Be honest, do you have any legalistic tendencies?

In 1 Peter 1:14, we are challenged, "Do not be conformed to the desires of your former ignorance." One of the ways we go back to our "former ignorance" is by trying to rely on our own power to live out the Christian life. Often, people will trust God to save them by His power, but then they'll try to follow Him for the rest of their lives by their own.

Holiness is more than a halo; it's also avoiding legalism.

The work of God is a start to finish process. He loves you so much that He wants you just how you are, but He also loves you so much that He isn't going to leave you that way. You're saved by His power, you're changed by His power, you live by His power, and one day, you'll be in heaven by His power. It's all a complete work of God.

Read Philippians 1:6 and fill in the blanks.

"I am sure of this, that he who _____ a good _____ in you will carry it on to _____ until the day of Christ _____."

PRAYER MOVEMENTS

HANDS UP
A sign of surrender.

- **Read Exodus 15:11.**

Spend time reflecting on the holiness of God. There is no one like Him. **Surrender** to the reality of who He is today, and do what this verse says—revere Him with praises.

HANDS OPEN
A sign of emptying out.

- **Read Leviticus 11:45.**

The Lord who brought you out of the captivity of slavery to sin is holy, so He is calling you to be holy. **Empty out** by confessing anything that is not holy. Ask God to remove it by His power.

HANDS OUT
A sign of receiving.

- **Read 1 Corinthians 1:30.**

The power of change comes from being in Christ Jesus. **Receive** this wisdom from God today. He is your righteousness, sanctification, and redemption.

HOLINESS IS BEING TRANSFORMED FROM THE INSIDE OUT

What would you do if I offered you a piece of candy, opened the wrapper, took out the candy, gave you the empty wrapper, and kept the piece of candy?

What would be your reaction if that happened to you?

Even though the wrapper is really attractive and colorful, you want what is on the inside more than what it's wrapped in.

READ MATTHEW 6:19-24.

Jesus taught a valuable lesson in Matthew 6:19-24. He said plainly that God cares about what's on the inside. Many people spend their whole lives trying to make their wrappers as attractive and colorful as possible, while neglecting to focus on what really matters—their soul. Too many people are chasing the wrapper—the best score, the best car, the best clothes, the most money, and on and on.

Why are people so obsessed with outward appearances?

How sad the day will be for someone to appear in front of God trying to present Him with an empty wrapper. Put your time, energy, and devotion into what is on the inside. Remember, your "wrapper" stays here; your soul goes on!

Do you tend to care more about what's on the inside or the outside when it comes to your own life? Why?

Holiness is more than a halo; it's being transformed from the inside out.

There is no shortcut to being transformed from the inside out. It comes with spiritual maturity through spending time with God. Being in the Word and praying is the best way to do that. When what's on the inside makes its way to the outside, that's when we'll see a movement of God.

PRAYER MOVEMENTS

HANDS UP
A sign of surrender.

- **Read 1 Samuel 2:2.**

Take a moment and reflect on your Holy God being a rock. There is no one like Him. **Surrender** to the truth that He is sturdy and strong when nothing else is. Stand firm in Him today.

HANDS OPEN
A sign of emptying out.

- **Read Leviticus 20:26.**

The Lord did the work to set us apart from the world around us. **Empty out** by confessing the areas of your life that don't look any different from those who don't follow Jesus. Ask Him to continue to change you by His power.

HANDS OUT
A sign of receiving.

- **Read Colossians 1:26.**

Jesus did the work to change your identity through the cross and resurrection. **Receive** the truth of who you are. Culture wants you to label yourself, but all that matters is who Jesus says you are. Let that truth determine how you live today.

HOLINESS IS LIVING DIFFERENTLY EVEN WHEN IT'S NOT POPULAR

READ MATTHEW 8:28-34.

Why are some people scared of Jesus changing them or the culture around them?

By the power of God, the sick are healed, the blind can see, the deaf can hear, and the lost are found. At the name of Jesus, the alcoholic gives up drinking forever, the drug abuser becomes clean, the sexually immoral person stops and waits for their future spouse, and the grump becomes a kind-hearted and compassionate person. Jesus changes people to go live differently in the world around them and be a witness for Him.

What is one specific thing in your life that Jesus has changed?

In Matthew 8:34, the people of the region of Gadarenes were outraged because Jesus had cast demons into their herd of pigs. They ignored what He had done for the two men and were more concerned about the animals. Jesus had healed these individuals when no one else could, but the people still didn't care.

However, two thousand years later there is still outrage toward Jesus. The sales of alcohol, pornography, and drugs go down when God is at work in people's lives. Yet, there is resistance to Him at every turn.

What has prepared you to live a holy life, even if it upsets other people?

Holiness is more than a halo; it's living differently in the world around you even when it's not popular.

Even though people may not realize it or even like it, they desperately need Jesus. Your school, your family, your sports team, your marching band, and your friends are all desperate for Jesus. Living differently by walking in holiness is the most effective way to bring His kingdom into those environments no matter how tough the opposition gets.

PRAYER MOVEMENTS

HANDS UP
A sign of surrender.

- **Read Isaiah 6:3.**

Surrender today to the authority of the Lord. Be reminded that there is no one like Him. Take a moment and listen to your favorite worship song. Sing along. Worship Him.

HANDS OPEN
A sign of emptying out.

- **Read Romans 12:1.**

Are there things that you're using your body for that aren't holy? **Empty out** by confessing any unholy things that you've been doing. Reject the mindset that tells you there's no point in trying to change now that you've already messed up. God rescues, redeems, and restores.

HANDS OUT
A sign of receiving.

- **Read 2 Corinthians 5:21.**

Never forget that Jesus did for you what you could never do for yourself. **Receive** the promise of the righteousness of God. Whether you've been a follower of Jesus for a few days or a long time, you need to be reminded of the gospel every day. Walk in that holiness today.

[HOLINESS IS PUTTING ON NEW CHARACTERISTICS]

READ COLOSSIANS 3:12-14.

Describe your favorite shirt that you wear the most.

Paul told the Colossians to put on certain characteristics (almost like clothes), so the people around them would know who they belonged to. Revival launches God's people to live differently in the world around them, so much so that unbelievers will often ask them why they act so differently. This is the ultimate opportunity to point them to a holy God that changes people.

However, before Paul gave them the list of characteristics to put on, he reminded them of their identity. Paul often followed this pattern in his letters. He would remind his audience who they were, then explain what they must do. He addressed identity before he addressed activity.

What are the three things Paul said we are in verse 12?

1.   2.   3.

What are eight characteristics Paul said to "put on" in verses 12-14?

1.   4.   7.

2.   5.   8.

3.   6.

Of those eight characteristics, which do you feel is your strongest?

Of those eight characteristics, which do you feel is your weakest?

Holiness is more than a halo; it's putting on new characteristics.

God calls us to holy living. However, this is only possible through the empowerment of the Holy Spirit.

PRAYER MOVEMENTS

HANDS UP
A sign of surrender.

- **Read Ezekiel 38:23.**

Spend time praying to the Lord and being reminded of His mission to make Himself known to the nations. **Surrender** to the call on your life to live differently in a way that people want to know your God.

HANDS OPEN
A sign of emptying out.

- **Read Hebrews 12:14.**

Remember, God is sending you out to make Him known in your daily mission fields. Godly characteristics will help you truly love others and will often provide opportunities to share the gospel. **Empty out** by confessing characteristics that are not in line with the characteristics God is calling you to.

HANDS OUT
A sign of receiving.

- **Read 2 Timothy 1:9.**

God has called you to live in holiness, which is to live differently in the world around you. **Receive** this call. What needs to change in your life? Don't try harder to be holy, trust in Him to make you holy and to give you holy characteristics.

SESSION 7: PASSION

IT'S MORE THAN ACTIVISM

Video Guide

KEY SCRIPTURE: Mark 6:41-44

1. Being an _____ is more than being on social media.

2. There's not a greater cause than the _____ _____ of Jesus.

3. Passion for Christ is the internal desire to _____ Jesus and to _____ Him so much that you want people to know Jesus too.

4. Jesus was the master of meeting people's _____ needs, so ultimately their _____ needs would be met as well.

5. A little bit in the hands of _____ is alway worth more than a whole lot in our own hands.

6. Revival happens when the _____ of God are passionate about God, passionate about people, and passionate about helping people meet _____.

7. The _____ way to serve people is to help them meet Jesus.

8. When we by faith place our _____, and our _____, and our _____ in the hands of Jesus, then they become eternally valuable.

Group Time

INFLUENCERS INFLUENCE OTHERS. What do Billy Graham (one of the most well-known evangelists of all time), Bill and Vonette Bright (founders of Campus Crusade for Christ), Jim Rayburn (founder of Young Life), Louis Evans, Jr. (President Ronald Reagan's former pastor), and Frederick Dale Bruner (a biblical scholar who wrote commentaries on Matthew and John) all have in common? They were all discipled and influenced by Dr. Henrietta C. Mears.

Henrietta lived from 1890-1963 and was a Christian educator who taught a Sunday school class for teens and college students every weekend in Baptist and Presbyterian churches. She was passionate about Jesus, the Bible, and empowering the next generation through Bible studies, leadership training, curriculum publishing, student camps, conferences, and missions.[1]

When you hear the word *influencer*, what comes to mind?

I'm guessing the number one answer would be someone on social media with thousands of followers and a blue verification check next to their name. However, a real influencer is someone who is passionate about impacting and influencing people to live the life that God intended for them.

> *"Teacher," as [Henrietta] was known by her 6,000-plus-member Sunday school class, would lean over the podium and, as if telling it for the first time, reiterate that "the Christian life is not 'trying to be good,' or 'trying to be like Jesus.' It is seeking to have a deeper experience of fellowship with Christ."*[2]

Even if very few people ever know your name, why should you still seek to be an influencer for Jesus?

Every "well-known" Christian leader or influencer was first impacted and influenced by someone. Millions have been influenced by the leaders Henrietta influenced. Most people have heard of Billy Graham, but very few have heard of Henrietta. However, her passion for the gospel influenced hundreds of people. Today, tens of thousands of additional disciples are now leading possible millions of people toward knowing Jesus.

What does the word *passion* mean to you?

Passion is an intense conviction that drives you. It's an internal feeling toward something or someone that is powerful enough to dictate your life and your desire to influence others toward the same conviction.

PASSION is more than activism or being cause-oriented. There is nothing wrong with being passionate about causes that serve and advocate for people made in God's image. However, our ultimate passion shouldn't be toward activism but toward the Lord Himself. Our goal as followers of Jesus isn't only to meet the needs people have for today but also to introduce people to the One who can meet their needs for eternity.

Why is it sometimes easier to be passionate about worshiping God than it is to be passionate about serving people?

A movement of God revives our passion for Jesus which leads to action.

BELIEVE IT & LIVE IT

READ MARK 6:34-44.

> [34] When he went ashore, he saw a large crowd and had compassion on them, because they were like sheep without a shepherd. Then he began to teach them many things. [35] When it grew late, his disciples approached him and said, "This place is deserted, and it is already late. [36] Send them away so that they can go into the surrounding countryside and villages to buy themselves something to eat." [37] "You

give them something to eat," he responded. They said to him, "Should we go and buy two hundred denarii worth of bread and give them something to eat?" ³⁸ He asked them, "How many loaves do you have? Go and see." When they found out they said, "Five, and two fish." ³⁹ Then he instructed them to have all the people sit down in groups on the green grass. ⁴⁰ So they sat down in groups of hundreds and fifties. ⁴¹ He took the five loaves and the two fish, and looking up to heaven, he blessed and broke the loaves. He kept giving them to his disciples to set before the people. He also divided the two fish among them all. ⁴² Everyone ate and was satisfied. ⁴³ They picked up twelve baskets full of pieces of bread and fish. ⁴⁴ Now those who had eaten the loaves were five thousand men. **MARK 6:34-44**

This account of Jesus feeding the five thousand is one of my favorite miracle stories in the Gospels. Besides the resurrection, this is the only miracle narrative that is told in all four Gospels: Matthew, Mark, Luke, and John. In fact, there were probably way more than five-thousand people there because they only accounted for the men. Many Bible scholars believe it would have been closer to fifteen or twenty-thousand people counting the women and children.

There is so much to learn from this story. One of the first things Mark reveals is that Jesus had compassion on the crowd (Mark 6:34). Literally, the word compassion means "to suffer together." It's a passion for another person's suffering that motivates you to help relieve that suffering.

> **Do you feel like the church is compassionate toward other people's suffering? What makes you feel that way?**

> **What about you personally? Are you compassionate toward suffering? Explain your answer.**

Jesus put His compassion into action with the ultimate purpose of pointing people to God. In fact, that it is the biblical strategy of missions. Missions has to be more than taking photos for Instagram or doing nice things for people. True missions meet physical needs, so you can meet a greater spiritual need. Physical solutions don't solve spiritual problems. However, sometimes, people can't hear our message of hope over the growling of their stomachs.

Meeting people's physical needs can help open ears to the gospel message. For example, we give bread to point to the Bread of Life. We give water to point to the Living Water. We paint fences to point to the gospel that can tear down walls. Jesus gave the perfect example of this model by giving hungry people food (vv. 41-42), so that He could feed spiritually hungry people spiritual food.

> Share a story where you served people to meet their physical needs, so you could share the gospel to meet their spiritual needs.

HOW DO YOU STAY PASSIONATE ABOUT THE RIGHT THINGS?

The best kind of passion is powered by God. What made this miracle so awesome was not the expanding of two fish sandwiches (five loaves and two fish), but rather, who actually performed the miracle. A little bit in the hands of Jesus is better than a whole lot in our hands.

READ JOHN 6:9-10.

9 "There's a boy here who has five barley loaves and two fish—but what are they for so many?" 10 Jesus said, "Have the people sit down." JOHN 6:9-10

Here is a young boy (another example where God uses young people to do extraordinary things), who donates his Lunchable. He could have kept it for himself. He could have easily thought, *What will I eat? Everyone else should have planned ahead. Not my problem.* Instead, he practiced compassion and gave it to serve others.

What would you have done if you were the young boy in this story? Donated your lunch or sneaked off to eat it by yourself?

His simple offering has been known for two thousand years, but it's also a beautiful picture of true kingdom service and passion. God used someone everyone else overlooked to perform a miracle. Everyone knows the story, and no one knows his name. The point of the kingdom of God is not to make much of our name but to make much of Jesus's name.

> "As long as we are content to live without revival, we will."[3]
> LEONARD RAVENHILL

May we stop being content with just going through the motions of religious activity with no real passion or life change. Real passion leads to real action. A movement of God happens when the Lord stirs hearts toward a real and healthy passion. What do we do with that passion? By faith and obedience, place it in the hands of Jesus. Our passion for Jesus, our passion for serving others, and our passion for advancing the gospel can only be effectively done through the power of the Holy Spirit.

Your life and passion in your own hands has value, because you're made in the image of God. However, if through faith and obedience, you place your life and passion in the hands of Jesus—that changes everything. Now, it has eternal value and an eternal impact. Why? Because, Jesus knows what to do with your life and passion in His hands.

Take an honest evaluation: Who's hands are your life and passion in right now? Your own hands or the hands of Jesus? How do you know?

[PASSION IS HELPING PEOPLE HEAR ABOUT JESUS]

READ JOHN 4:39-42.

Have you ever shared the gospel with someone who didn't know Jesus? What happened?

Every single one of us can come up with excuses listing why we don't serve other people or share the gospel with them.

What are some common excuses that you've heard others use, or that you have used yourself?

If we are honest with ourselves, we have all had a defeated mindset about sharing the gospel with others at some point in the past. However, the truth is that one person can make all the difference in the world.

In John 4, Jesus approached a Samaritan woman who was radically changed by Him. This single woman goes and tells her entire town about the Man who told her everything she ever did (v. 39). She did not do anything to change their hearts, but she introduced them to the One who could.

When have you seen one person make a difference?

One person can make a difference. Will you be willing to say, "Okay, God, even if I am by myself, I will be your witness"? Realize that the pressure is off your shoulders because you can't change anyone by yourself. Only Christ can do that.

Passion is more than activism; it's helping people hear about Jesus.

READ 2 CORINTHIANS 5:20.

The greatest passion and action you can have is to be a passionate and active ambassador for Christ!

PRAYER MOVEMENTS

HANDS UP
A sign of surrender.

- **Read Job 9:4.**

Spend time praying to the Lord and being reminded of His power. There is no one that can beat Him. He always wins. Your passion needs to be connected to His victorious power. **Surrender** to the call on your life to make Him known in your daily mission field.

HANDS OPEN
A sign of emptying out.

- **Read 1 John 4:8.**

Remember, God is sending you out to make Him known in your daily mission fields. Having compassion for people comes from having the love of God inside of you. **Empty out** by confessing any indifference you have toward people. Ask God to replace indifference with His compassion and love for others.

HANDS OUT
A sign of receiving.

- **Read 1 John 4:9.**

God has called you to live with a passion for knowing Him and making Him known. **Receive** God's love through the power of the gospel, and ask Him to love others through you by serving them and sharing the gospel.

[PASSION IS VALUING THE RIGHT PERSON ABOVE ALL]

READ MARK 2:23-28.

What good things in the church do we tend to be more passionate about than Jesus?

Have you ever heard the saying, "too much of a good thing"? Sometimes, this old proverb can be very true. For instance, exercise is good for you, but an excessive amount with no rest can be unhealthy. We know food is good in moderation, but too much ice cream all at once can make you feel sick.

A good thing can also be very dangerous when it's used in a wrong or legalistic way. As Christians, we can fall prey to worshiping instruments used in praising God, instead of God Himself. Sometimes, we are guilty of becoming trapped by certain music styles, worship orders, or ministry techniques. Other times, we may even enjoy the acts of ministry or serving others more than we enjoy spending time with Jesus. If you're not careful, it's incredibly easy to fall more in love with the things of God than God Himself.

Has there ever been a time when you valued and enjoyed the things of God more than God Himself?

In Mark 2:23-28, the Pharisees had become so legalistic that they had turned the Sabbath day into a burdensome kind of straitjacket. Jesus told the Pharisees that the Sabbath is not a day created for its own sake—it's a gift from God as a day of rest to meditate and worship Him.

Passion is more than activism; it's valuing the right Person above all.

It's okay to enjoy certain styles over others. However, if you feel like you can't worship God because of certain ministry or worship styles, then you may need to repent of being more passionate about the things of God than God Himself. Realize that music, church services, and teaching styles are ultimately just instruments and gifts by God to worship Him.

How can you grow in your passion for Jesus above all?

PRAYER MOVEMENTS

HANDS UP
A sign of surrender.

- **Read Jeremiah 10:10.**

Spend time reflecting on how great the Lord is. He is a God of love, but He is also a God of wrath. **Surrender** to His Lordship today. Be passionate about Him, knowing that if you belong to Him, you'll never experience His wrath, because Jesus did that on the cross in your place.

HANDS OPEN
A sign of emptying out.

- **Read Colossians 3:23.**

The greatest passion you can have is for the Lord by serving Him and others from your heart. **Empty out** by confessing anything that you're currently more passionate about than Jesus.

HANDS OUT
A sign of receiving.

- **Read 1 John 3:16.**

Jesus set the example for us. His passion and compassion led Him to lay His life down for you. **Receive** this example today to be reminded of His love for you, but also His example to go and show compassion toward others.

[PASSION IS HELPING THOSE AROUND YOU]

READ MARK 3:1-6.

In today's text, we find Jesus in opposition to the Pharisees once again because of the Sabbath day. He had come across a man with a withered hand and healed him. The only response we see from the Pharisees is absolute disgust in Jesus performing this miracle on the Sabbath. The Sabbath is a good thing. It was a gift that God gave people as a day of rest. However, the day or the gift was never meant to be more important than people.

Why is it easier to promote a cause on social media than it is to actually help and serve the people around us?

There are a few things we need to recognize in these verses. First, the man with the withered hand was in the synagogue, a place where people were supposed to come for healing and compassion. The Pharisees ignored him because it was the Sabbath. Second, when Jesus asked them whether or not He should heal the man, they stood silent. Christ was angered and grieved by the hardness of their hearts. Lastly, the Pharisees valued their traditions more than people.

There is a term that has become popular over the recent years—*slacktivism*. Basically, slacktivism is the passion of supporting political or social causes mainly online but not really doing anything about it in your personal life.

What is an example of slacktivism that you've seen?

For example, I often wonder how many social media posts are typed out for some cause, compared to the number of gospel conversations being shared with a spiritually lost person or serving someone in need. After all, the greatest cause is making disciples and loving your neighbor as yourself.

Passion is more than activism; it's actually helping those around you.

How can you focus more on what God is doing and calling you to, than the things you don't like going on around you?

Spend time today focusing on getting your priorities in order. Glorifying God and ministering to people is what Christianity is all about!

PRAYER MOVEMENTS

HANDS UP
A sign of surrender.

- **Read Psalm 37:4.**

There is nothing wrong with telling God what your needs are, but the order of this verse is very intentional and important. Take a moment to delight in the Lord. **Surrender** your delight to Him. Let your main passion be Him.

HANDS OPEN
A sign of emptying out.

- **Read 1 Corinthians 10:31.**

Everything we do should be about His glory. **Empty out** by confessing the areas of your life where you tend to be more passionate about your own glory than His.

HANDS OUT
A sign of receiving.

- **Read Mark 11:24.**

This verse doesn't mean God is going to do whatever you want. It means when His passion has become your passion, He will give you what you ask because it will line up with His will. **Receive** the calling today to go live out the things He is passionate about.

PASSION IS BEING ACTIVELY PLUGGED INTO THE POWER SOURCE

Recently, I got a new cell phone. When I took the new phone out of the box, it was absolutely dead and useless, until I plugged the charger into the phone. Power from an abundant source had to be transferred to this single source that lacked power. Once the phone was charged up from the power source, it began to work.

When have you been unable to use something because the battery was dead, or you didn't have access to electricity?

READ LUKE 8:43-48.

In Luke 8:43-48, a story is recorded about a woman who had been bleeding for twelve years. The woman reached out from a crowd and touched just the hem of the garment of the ultimate power source. Jesus knew that power had left Him. He wasn't saying that He had lost power, but that power had been transferred from Him to another source. The woman was immediately healed, and her life was changed forever!

When have you felt the power of God at work in you?

Passion is more than activism; it's being actively plugged into the Power Source.

It's easy to confuse real passion for emotions. It's often easy to stir up an emotional response to convince ourselves or others that we're passionate about something. However, you'll be a lot more effective operating with real passion that comes from being plugged into Him.

In 2 Corinthians 5:20, there is the promise that God is the power doing the work through us. Thank Him today that you serve a God who has the power to change lives. He is the ultimate Power Source who never loses any strength, no matter how many people He transfers it to.

How does a person operate in His power over their own?

PRAYER MOVEMENTS

HANDS UP
A sign of surrender.

- **Read Exodus 15:6.**

Surrender today to the reality of the power of the Lord. You don't worship a weak God off in the distance; you worship an all-powerful God, who is up close and personal and has defeated the enemy.

HANDS OPEN
A sign of emptying out.

- **Read Deuteronomy 8:17.**

We all tend to default to trying to do things by our own power. **Empty out** by confessing and repenting of trying to serve the Lord by your own power.

HANDS OUT
A sign of receiving.

- **Read 1 Chronicles 29:11.**

Rest in the truth that you don't have to generate passion by your own power. Slowly read and reflect on how this verse describes your Lord. **Receive** the promise of who He is and His power. Let your passion today be generated by His power source.

SESSION 8:
URGENCY

IT'S MORE THAN BEING BUSY FOR JESUS

Video Guide

KEY SCRIPTURE: Acts 1:8-11

1. Urgency is more than just being _____.

2. When God calls you to do something, _____ is the _____.

3. When the power of the Holy Spirit comes to live inside of us, it _____ everything.

4. You have one call on your life: to know _____ and to make Him known.

5. Now is the time to be the _____. Now is the time to go and know Jesus and make Jesus _____.

Group Time

Woodlawn: the true story that inspired a movie. In the early 1970s, in Birmingham, Alabama, there was a destructive amount of racial tension and unrest that would often generate violence. This fighting even spilled over into the high schools. However, in the midst of chaos, a spiritual awakening and movement of God took place among the students.

At Woodlawn High School in 1973, there was an African American athlete by the name of Tony Nathan. The high school football coach wanted Tony to be the varsity team's starting running back on a predominantly Caucasian football team. Unfortunately, in the early 1970s, this caused considerable backlash with many citizens of the southern town.

However, the head coach and the team chaplain believed there was an urgency to do what was right. They believed their ultimate calling was bigger than a game; it was teaching these teenagers about life, loving your neighbor, and, ultimately, eternal life.

What do you believe are the most important things in life?

Many of the players on the football team at Woodlawn High School were led to faith in Jesus Christ by the team chaplain. Soon, the opposing sides of the racial war could be seen fellowshipping together at home meetings through the Fellowship of Christian Athletes.[1] This movement soon spread across the school and entire community.

Are there opportunities at your school for Christian students to gather together? If so, what? If not, could God be calling you to lead?

Through revival and a spiritual awakening lead by teenagers, a once divided city began to find healing as they personally experienced the urgency of the gospel for themselves. They started sharing the gospel with others and acting like the church God had commanded them to be. These young people realized that God was calling them to do what actually mattered.

Do you believe it is possible for revival to come to your community? To your school? To your church? To your personal life?

Something urgent is of the utmost importance and requires swift action. Now is the time to wake up to what God is calling His people to. Now is the time for the gospel. Now is the time to be the church. Now is the time to go. Souls are at risk. An entire generation is desperate for Jesus, whether they know it or not.

Urgency is more than just doing busy work in Jesus's name; it's doing what He is actually calling us to without hesitation.

A movement of God happens when people wake up to the urgency of what God is calling them to—no longer being comfortable with complacency or busyness.

What are you allowing to act as a distraction from what God is actually asking you to do with urgency?

BELIEVE IT & LIVE IT

READ ACTS 1:3,8,9-11.

After he had suffered, he also presented himself alive to them by many convincing proofs, appearing to them over a period of forty days and speaking about the kingdom of God. **ACTS 1:3**

"But you will receive power when the Holy Spirit has come on you, and you will be my witnesses in Jerusalem, in all Judea and Samaria, and to the ends of the earth." **ACTS 1:8**

> [9] After he had said this, he was taken up as they were watching, and a cloud took him out of their sight. [10] While he was going, they were gazing into heaven, and suddenly two men in white clothes stood by them. [11] They said, "Men of Galilee, why do you stand looking up into heaven? This same Jesus, who has been taken from you into heaven, will come in the same way that you have seen him going into heaven."
>
> **ACTS 1:9-11**

As believers, filled and sealed by the Holy Spirit, we find our roots in the book of Acts. Luke (a physician and the author of the Gospel of Luke) wrote Acts to give an account of the birth of the church. Here in Acts 1 we see what our purpose is as believers and what the Lord is urgently calling us to.

What is Jesus calling His followers to do in Acts 1?

True revival is not emotionalism; it's an awakening of God's people to the calling on their lives. A movement of God happens when we finally get serious about doing what He is telling us to do with urgency.

Now is the time for the gospel. In Acts 1:3, Luke reminded his readers what the core truths of the gospel are. Jesus suffered (that's the crucifixion), but three days later, "he also presented himself alive… by many convincing proofs." Jesus lives! The tomb is empty, but seated on the throne is the risen King of kings and Lord of lords. Because the grave is empty, people can be full of the life of Christ. Jesus lives, so hope lives. Jesus lives, so peace lives. Jesus lives, so joy lives. Jesus lives, so love lives. Now is the time for you to experience the gospel for yourself and to urgently share this message with the world.

How would you articulate the full gospel to an unbeliever?

Now is the time to be the church. You may have seen Acts 1:8 on the back of a mission t-shirt before. However, it's more than a t-shirt verse; it's the last promise given by Jesus here on earth before He ascended into heaven. He said, "You will receive power when the Holy Spirit has come on you." Then, you will be His witness everywhere you go. This promise would be fulfilled in Acts 2.

What is the church? It is people who have been filled with the power of the Holy Spirit and have been called to be witnesses everywhere they go to accomplish the Great Commission (see Matt. 28:18-20). The church is not a building to be maintained; it is a people to be mobilized with urgency. Be the church now.

> How does this change your view of yourself realizing that you are the church right now?

HOW DO YOU LIVE WITH URGENCY?

Now is the time to go. In Acts 1:9-11, after Jesus ascended into heaven, the disciples were astonished and staring up at the clouds. Could you imagine being there? The disciples were probably extremely confused and asking, "What just happened?" It was the ultimate mic drop moment. Jesus gave the promise of Acts 1:8, then took off like a bottle rocket (v. 9).

As the disciples were gazing at the sky with their mouths hanging open in shock, two angels suddenly appeared and said, "Why do you stand looking up into heaven? This same Jesus, who has been taken from you into heaven, will come in the same way that you have seen him going into heaven" (Acts 1:10-11).

> What gives you confidence that this promise of Jesus's return will be fulfilled?

There will be a day when Jesus Christ returns to earth physically and visibly to bring a final judgment and to gather His church (those who have been born again). Some people get a little weird when it comes to the second coming, but it doesn't have to be that way. The return of Christ should be an encouragement for the believer and a warning for the unbeliever.

READ JOHN 14:3.

The eventual second coming of Jesus is a reality that should be fuel for missions and evangelism. As long as we have life and Christ has yet to return, then we have an opportunity to be the church that shares the gospel. However, the moment we draw our last breath (or Christ returns), it's too late.

> When is a revival needed? When carelessness and unconcern keep the people asleep.[2]
>
> BILLY SUNDAY

Now is the time for the church to wake up and go with urgency. Now is the time for the gospel. Now is the time to be the church. Now is the time to go. Never give up, back up, or shut up until Jesus calls us up.

Where is God calling you to go with urgency and to be the church by taking the gospel there?

CLOSING PRAYER

Father, we want to go with urgency, sharing Your gospel with a world that desperately needs it. Help us to be a revival generation, desiring for nothing less than our friends and family to know You as their Lord and King. Amen.

TIME WITH JESUS

For the last three Times with Jesus, focus only on prayer. Don't go through the motions. Truly surrender, empty out, and receive what God wants to give you. Be silent before Him, and allow Him to speak to you. Remember, revival always begins with prayer. May it be that the time you have spent in this study and in prayer will spark a revival in you that turns into an inferno that helps spark a revival in your generation.

PRAYER MOVEMENTS

HANDS OPEN
A sign of emptying out.

"And let us consider one another in order to provoke love and good works, not neglecting to gather together, as some are in the habit of doing, but encouraging each other, and all the more as you see the day approaching." Hebrews 10:24-25

Are you avoiding the church? Are you gathering with fellow believers? **Empty out** by confessing anything that is getting in the way of church being a priority to you.

HANDS UP
A sign of surrender.

"God has spoken once; I have heard this twice: strength belongs to God." Psalm 62:11

Spend time reflecting on how strong the Lord is. Tell Him how you need Him and His strength to be with you while you're in your daily mission field. **Surrender** to His calling to go with urgency.

HANDS OUT
A sign of receiving.

"Until now you have asked for nothing in my name. Ask and you will receive, so that your joy may be complete." John 16:24

How often are you going through your day without going to God in prayer? **Receive** this promise from God that He wants you to come to Him. Pray before you go in urgency.

PRAYER MOVEMENTS

HANDS UP
Sign of surrender.

"He alone does great wonders. His faithful love endures forever." Psalm 136:4

Take a moment and reflect on how great God really is. **Surrender** to the truth—He is better than any idols that may distract you from what He is calling you to.

HANDS OPEN
A sign of emptying out.

"I am saying this for your own benefit, not to put a restraint on you, but to promote what is proper and so that you may be devoted to the Lord without distraction." 1 Corinthians 7:35

If the enemy can't get you to sin, he will just try to distract you. **Empty out** by confessing the things that are distracting and keeping you from doing what God is calling you to do as the church.

HANDS OUT
A sign of receiving.

"For we are God's coworkers. You are God's field, God's building." 1 Corinthians 3:9

Remember who you are now because of the work of the gospel in your life. **Receive** this truth today and live by walking in obedience to whatever He is calling you to today with urgency.

PRAYER MOVEMENTS

HANDS UP
A sign of surrender.

"He counts the number of the stars; he gives names to all of them."
Psalm 147:4

Surrender today to the truth that if God has given all the stars names, then He remembers your name. By obedience, trust that when He sends you out with urgency, He is going with you. Pray and ask the King to show you at least one person in your life today that does not know Him.

HANDS OPEN
A sign of emptying out.

"And God is able to make every grace overflow to you, so that in every way, always having everything you need, you may excel in every good work." 2 Corinthians 9:8

What hesitations do you have today about being sent to go and be the church? **Empty out** by confessing fear or excuses. A friend of mine says, "God pays for what He orders." Meaning, if God has called you to it, He will resource you to do it. There are no excuses.

HANDS OUT
A sign of receiving.

"And remember, I am with you always, to the end of the age." Matthew 28:20

Lastly, ask the Spirit to help you trust and obey His presence in you. **Receive** the calling on your life to go where He is sending you to make Him known. The Spirit in us wants to see a revival and spiritual awakening, even more than we do. Walk in that obedience today.

LEADER GUIDE

LEADING A GROUP?

We have what you need to lead a group of students through *Revival Generation*. Visit lifeway.com/revivalgeneration for free leader downloads, promotional resources, and more. Leader kits are also available and include a copy of the book and access codes to the digital videos.

The following is a guide for a leading students through *Revival Generation*. Feel free to personalize this schedule to fit the needs of your group.

GROUP TIME SCHEDULE

- Recap the previous session (5 minutes)
- Watch the teaching video from author, Shane Pruitt (6-8 minutes)
- Opening activity (5 minutes)
- Group discussion (25-30 minutes)
- Close in prayer (5 minutes)

TIPS TO LEADING A GROUP

- Do the study alongside students. Make notes as you work through the Times with Jesus and bring those thoughts to your group time.
- Gather any supplies for games or activities before the group meets.
- Cue up the video with Shane Pruitt prior to students gathering for group time.
- Don't be afraid of silence. Students need time to process and think, especially after a deep question.
- Record prayer requests and follow up.
- Pray for students throughout the week.

SESSION 1

Introduction: Make sure everyone in the group knows one another. Allow students to share their names, grade, where they go to school, and an interesting fact about themselves.

Video Guide: Watch the video and encourage students to take notes as they follow along.

Opening Activity: Take a few minutes and direct students to come up with a definition for "revival." They can do it individually or as a group, but write their definition on a whiteboard or sticky note. Then say, "This Bible study is all about revival. I'm not going to define it for you now, but over the next eight weeks, we'll learn exactly what revival is and isn't."

Main Point: Revival is more than a feeling; it's an awakening.

Key Scripture: Acts 2:42-47

Session Summary:
- The world of the Jesus Revolution of the 1960s is similar to today.
- God did a work then. Could He do it again today?
- True revival is God's people getting serious about worshiping Him above all and living out their true purpose of knowing Him and making Him known.
- The events that occurred from Jesus's death, resurrection, ascension, and the coming of the Holy Spirit sparked the movement of God that launched the church.
- Changed lives change the world around them.
- Revival cannot be manipulated, but we can have prepared hearts if God chooses to pour out revival on us.

Prayer: Close your session in prayer. Ask for prayer needs, and encourage students to complete their Times with Jesus for the week.

SESSION 2

Recap: Remind students that the previous session revolved around revival not being about feelings but a true spiritual awakenings. Ask students to share any insights they may have had during their Time with Jesus.

Video Guide: Watch the video and encourage students to take notes as they follow along.

Opening Activity: Divide the group into two teams. Use a streaming service or YouTube to create a playlist of popular worship songs. Play the first few seconds of the song and see which team can name the song the quickest. Play four to six songs. End the challenge with my favorite worship song, "Clear the Stage," by Ross King. Search the internet for copies of the lyrics to the song and distribute them to the students for a follow-up activity.

Main Point: Revival, or a movement of God in our lives, will stir us to lay down our idols and worship God alone.

Key Scripture: Jeremiah 10:1-10

Session Summary:
- Worship is more than music.
- Worship is placing your highest adoration and affection on someone or something.
- God called Israel to have no other gods or idols before Him and used Jeremiah to proclaim this message to the people. However, Israel slipped into idolatry.
- We are born knowing how to worship; we just need to worship the right One.
- Nothing else in our lives will make us whole apart from Jesus.
- Personal revival is experienced when we clear the sage of our hearts and make space for the only One who deserves our worship.

Prayer: Close your session in prayer. Ask for prayer needs, and encourage students to complete their Times with Jesus for the week.

SESSION 3

Recap: Remind students that the previous session revolved around worship and how we need to clear our lives of idols. Ask students to share any insights they may have had during their Time with Jesus.

Video Guide: Watch the video and encourage students to take notes as they follow along.

Opening Activity: Give everyone a piece of paper and a pen. Ask students to write down some things in their lives that they know aren't pleasing to God. This is for their eyes only, and they will not be asked to share. When they are finished, ask them to fold their paper and put it in the back of their Bible, book, or someplace where it won't be seen. At the end of the session, give students a chance to repent of these things and destroy that piece of paper.

Main Point: Revival is often preceded by repentance. When God changes our hearts and minds, He will also change our actions.

Key Scripture: Acts 19:11-20

Session Summary:
- Part of repentance is confessing sin and apologizing to God, but that's not all of it.
- There are two types of repentance: initial repentance at salvation and a lifestyle of ongoing repentance that comes with following Jesus.
- Fans of Jesus don't allow Him to change their lives. Followers of Jesus see Him as the Lord of their lives who has say over everything.
- The seven sons of Sceva were fans of Jesus who had no authority over demons.
- The people of Ephesus genuinely repented and destroyed their magic books.
- A lifestyle of repentance is a constant realization that Jesus is better than anything else we might pursue.

Closing Illustration: Remind students about the things they wrote on their piece of paper at the beginning of the session. As a sign of repentance, have them ball the paper up and throw it away, tear it up into tiny pieces, and dispose of it. Remind students of Psalm 103:12, "As far as the east is from the west, so far has he removed our transgressions from us."

Prayer: Close your session in prayer. Ask for prayer needs, and encourage students to complete their Times with Jesus for the week.

SESSION 4

Recap: Remind students that the previous session revolved around repentance and how it's more than just feeling sorry for our sin. Ask students to share any insights they may have had during their Time with Jesus.

Video Guide: Watch the video and encourage students to take notes as they follow along.

Opening Activity: Place a chair that students can safely stand on in front of the group. Say, "We can say we believe that this chair exists because we can see it. We can even believe that this chair will hold us up if we sit or stand on it. However, the only way to show faith in the chair is to exercise trust by actually sitting or standing on it." Ask for a volunteer to reveal their trust by sitting in the chair. Faith is always tied to trust.

Main Point: Revival happens when the Spirit awakens you to how big He really is, so that you will have a big faith in a big God.

Key Scripture: Acts 5:27-42

Session Summary:
- Just believing in God doesn't make you a follower of Jesus.
- Spiritual awakening occurs when we don't fully understand everything going on around us, and we still trust Him.
- The disciples displayed faith in Jesus even in the face of harsh opposition.
- Movements started by humans will eventually fail. Movements that are powered by God cannot be stopped.
- The disciples realized they had an all-powerful, nothing-is-impossible God living inside of them, and that made them fearless.

Prayer: Close your session in prayer. Ask for prayer needs, and encourage students to complete their Times with Jesus for the week.

SESSION 5

Recap: Remind students that the previous session revolved around faith and how it's more than simply believing that God exists. Ask students to share any insights they may have had during their Time with Jesus.

Video Guide: Watch the video and encourage students to take notes as they follow along.

Opening Activity: Play Simon Says, but go as fast as possible. So that you don't draw a blank when you're calling out commands from Simon, write some commands down before the group meets. (Play for three to five minutes. It's always best to stop playing a game while it's still fun.)

When you are finished playing, tie in that the point of the game is to obey Simon. Explain that Simon is just a made-up figure in a game; no one knows who Simon really is! However, there is a real Savior that is calling us to obedience, and He is much greater and better than any "Simon" in any game we could play.

Main Point: A movement of God happens when the people of God start living in full obedience to their God.

Key Scripture: Isaiah 6:1-8

Session Summary:
- The life of Annie Armstrong revealed what God can do with someone who is obedient to Him.
- Obedience is hearing the calling of God on your life and acting on it.
- Isaiah recorded seeing a vision of the King who cleansed him of his sins and called him to a mission.
- When God saves us, it's not just to get out of hell for free. He saves us to a relationship, a mission, a purpose in life, and to obedience.
- Revival comes when God's people live a life of obedience to Him.

Prayer: Close your session in prayer. Ask for prayer needs, and encourage students to complete their Times with Jesus for the week.

SESSION 6

Recap: Remind students that the previous session revolved around obedience and how it's more than a "get out of hell free" card. Ask students to share any insights they may have had during their Time with Jesus.

Video Guide: Watch the video and encourage students to take notes as they follow along.

Opening Activity: Before the session, write out a pair of cards for several different types of animals, such as dogs, cats, chickens, and goats. As students arrive, give them each a card with an animal on it. Make sure there are two cards for each animal you chose. Direct students to start making the sound associated with the animal on their card until they find their match. After everyone has found their partner, ask the question: If you started a zoo, what is the very first animal you would get? Why? If time permits, allow students to share their answers. Use this activity to introduce the story of the Welsh Revival on page 91.

Main Point: A movement of God in your life doesn't mean you'll be perfect. However, the desire and power to live in holiness should be evident.

Key Scripture: 1 Peter 1:13-17

Session Summary:
- When a revival swept across Wales in the early 1900s, lives were so changed that the donkeys had to be retrained because they only knew commands using cuss words.
- Holiness is being set apart by God to live differently from the world around us.
- Peter reminded his readers that the Holy Spirit lived inside of them and was propelling them to be more like Christ every day.
- Over time, your character and love should begin to look more and more like His.
- Biblical holiness comes from the overflow of your identity in Christ and the power of the Holy Spirit.
- It truly is a journey of learning about the holiness of God and how to be who He made you to be, which will translate into holy living.

Prayer: Close your session in prayer. Ask for prayer needs, and encourage students to complete their Times with Jesus for the week.

SESSION 7

Recap: Remind students that the previous session revolved around holiness and how it's not about perfection but allowing the Holy Spirit to change us. Ask students to share any insights they may have had during their Time with Jesus.

Video Guide: Watch the video and encourage students to take notes as they follow along.

Opening Activity: Go around the room and ask each student to answer this question: Who has had the biggest impact on your life? Explain why you chose this person.

Main Point: A movement of God revives our passion for Jesus which leads to action.

Key Scripture: Mark 6:34-44

Session Summary:

- Passion is an intense conviction that drives you. It's an internal feeling toward something or someone and is so powerful that it dictates your life and your desire to influence others toward the same conviction. It's more than activism.
- In feeding the five thousand, Jesus met their physical needs in order to meet their deeper spiritual needs.
- A little bit in the hands of Jesus is better than a whole lot in our hands.
- The point of the kingdom of God is not to make much of our name but to make much of Jesus's name.
- Real passion leads to real action. A movement of God happens when the Lord stirs hearts toward a real and healthy passion.

Closing Illustration: With a basketball in your hand, mention that a basketball is worth about twenty-five dollars. However, if you place that same ball in Michael Jordan's hands, Steph Curry's hands, LeBron James's hands? Now it's worth millions. It's the same with your life. Your life and passion in your own hands has value, because you're made in the image of God. However, if through faith and obedience, you place your life and passion in the hands of Jesus—that changes everything. Now, it has eternal value and an eternal impact. Why? Because, Jesus knows what to do with your life and passion in His hands. Challenge students to take an honest evaluation and ask: Who's hands are your life and passion in right now? Your own hands or the hands of Jesus? How do you know?

Prayer: Close your session in prayer. Ask for prayer needs, and encourage students to complete their Times with Jesus for the week.

SESSION 8

Recap: Remind students that the previous session revolved around passion and how it's more than activism or causes. Ask students to share any insights they may have had during their Time with Jesus.

Video Guide: Watch the video and encourage students to take notes as they follow along.

Opening Activity: Before the group meets, list eight to ten famous movie quotes, like "I'm the king of the world!" or "I am Iron Man." Give each person a piece of paper and a pen to record their answers, then read the quotes out loud one at a time. After you've read all the movie quotes, see who correctly guessed the most movie titles. Then, give everyone an opportunity to answer the question: What is your favorite movie, and why is it your favorite?

Main Point: A movement of God happens when people wake up to the urgency of what God is calling them to, and no longer being comfortable with complacency or busyness.

Key Scripture: Acts 1:3,8,9-11

Session Summary:
- The movie *Woodlawn* portrays a group of students who felt the urgency of the gospel to love each other, influencing their entire community for Jesus.
- Urgency is more than just doing busy work in Jesus's name; it's doing what He is actually calling us to without hesitation.
- A movement of God happens when we finally get serious about doing what He is telling us to do with urgency. Now is the time.
- Now is the time for you to experience the gospel for yourself with urgency and to go share this message with the world.
- The church is not a building to be maintained; it is a people to be mobilized.
- The return of Christ should be an encouragement for the believer and a warning for the unbeliever.
- For a great tool to utilize in sharing the gospel, download the Life on Mission app.

Prayer: Close your session in prayer. Ask for prayer needs, and encourage students to complete their Times with Jesus for the week.

ENDNOTES

SESSION 1

1. Stephen F. Olford, "The Pattern for Revival," *Herald of His Coming* (1998), https://heraldofhiscoming.org/index.php/read-the-herald/past-issues/310-past-issues/1998/sep98/3494-the-pattern-for-revival-9-98.
2. Andrew Whitman, "Jesus Revolution: The 60s Hippies Who Changed the World," *Premier Christianity*, March 19, 2023, https://www.premierchristianity.com/home/the-jesus-people-revolution-the-60s-hippies-who-changed-the-world/3787.article.
3. Stephen F. Olford, "The Pattern for Revival."
4. "High Kicks Meet High Fashion: The Most Expensive Sneakers Of All Time," *Luxe Digital*, February 2, 2023, https://luxe.digital/lifestyle/style/most-expensive-sneakers/.

SESSION 2

1. John T. McNeill (ed.), *Calvin: Institutes of the Christian Religion, vol. 1* (Philadelphia: The Westminster Press, 1960).
2. Ross King, "Clear the Stage," *Northpaw Music*, 2002.

SESSION 3

1. Anne Graham Lotz (@AGLotz), "Revival begins when you draw a circle around yourself and make sure everything in that circle is right with God.", *Twitter*, July 25, 2014, https://twitter.com/aglotz/status/492608973397557248.
2. Kyle Idleman, *Not a Fan: Becoming a Completely Committed Follower of Jesus* (Grand Rapids, MI: Zondervan, 2011), 25.
3. Anne Graham Lotz, *Twitter*.

SESSION 4

1. Leonard Ravenhill, *Why Revival Tarries* (Minneapolis, MN: Bethany House Publishers, 1959), 40.

SESSION 5

1. Selma Ulmer, "Annie Armstrong: The 'Mastermind' behind WMU," *Women's Missionary Union*, March 5, 2021, https://wmu.com/annie-armstrong-the-mastermind-behind-wmu/.
2. Ibid.
3. Ibid.
4. Ibid.
5. For more information on the Annie Armstrong Easter Offering, check out www.anniearmstrong.com.

6. Steven Lawson, "How Were People Saved in the Old Testament?" *Ligonier*, https://www.ligonier.org/learn/qas/how-were-people-saved-in-the-old-testament.

7. Greg Laurie & Ellen Vaughn, *Jesus Revolution* (Grand Rapids, MI: Baker Books, 2018), 243.

SESSION 6

1. William Stead, "Revival Swept Across Wales," *Christianity*, May 3, 2010, https://www.christianity.com/church/church-history/timeline/1901-2000/revival-swept-across-wales-11630678.html.

2. Ibid.

3. Elmer Towns & Douglas Porter, *The Ten Greatest Revivals Ever* (Ann Arbor, MI: Servant Publications, 2000), 25.

4. J. Edwin Orr, *The Flaming Tongue: Evangelical Awakenings, 1900* (Chicago, IL: Moody Publishing, 1975), 192-193.

5. Wayne Grudem, *Tyndale New Testament Commentary: 1 Peter* (Leicester, England: Inter-Varsity Press, 1988), 79.

6. Ibid, 79.

7. Scott Pace and Shane Pruitt, *Calling Out the Called: Discipling Those Called to Ministry Leadership* (Nashville, TN: B & H Publishing, 2022).

8. J. I. Packer, *Your Father Loves You* (Wheaton, IL: Harold Shaw Publishers, 1986).

SESSION 7

1. Arlin C. Migliazzo, "Henriatta Mears, the Improbable Evangelical Leader," *Christianity Today*, December 13, 2021, https://www.christianitytoday.com/ct/2022/january-february/henrietta-mears-improbable-leader-teacher-migliazzo.html.

2. Ibid.

3. "Leonard Ravenhill Quotes," *Goodreads*, n.d., https://www.goodreads.com/author/quotes/159020.Leonard_Ravenhill.

SESSION 8

1. Suzanne Niles, "Director Jon Erwin Shares the Amazing True Story Behind 'Woodlawn,'" *Sonoma Christian Home*, October 28, 2015, https://sonomachristianhome.com/2015/10/director-jon-erwin-shares-the-amazing-true-story-behind-woodlawn/.

2. Billy Sunday, "The Need for Revivals," *Prayer Leader*, n.d., https://www.prayerleader.com/classics-5/.

Get the most from your study.

Promotional videos and other leader materials available at
lifeway.com/revivalgeneration.

Our world is divided in almost every way imaginable—religion, politics,
race, views on sexuality, and much, much more. On the surface, it
might not seem like the time is right for a movement of God. On
the contrary, now is the perfect time for revival. Not the emotional,
momentary, feel-good type that comes and goes, but a revival that
changes hearts. When God changes hearts, churches change. And
changed churches change cities, which change nations, which change
the world. When the world has seemed to be at its darkest, the Spirit of
God has moved in a way that only He could. Can He do it again? Yes,
He can. We just need to prepare our hearts to be ready when He does.

In this eight-session Bible study, Shane Pruitt will explore eight words
associated with revival, including worship, repentance, obedience,
and more. He will explain what revival is and what it is not. Revival is
more than a feeling; it's a movement of God!

Want to watch the *Revival Generation* teaching videos when and
where it's most convenient? Introducing the Lifeway On Demand app!
From your smartphone to your TV, watching videos from Lifeway has
never been easier. Visit lifeway.com/revivalgeneration or the Lifeway
on Demand app to purchase the teaching videos and hear from author
Shane Pruitt.

For more information about Lifeway Students, visit lifeway.com/students.

ADDITIONAL RESOURCES

**REVIVAL GENERATION VIDEO
STREAMING BUNDLE**
Eight teaching videos
from author, Shane Pruitt.
Available at lifeway.com/
revivalgeneration.

**REVIVAL GENERATION
LEADER KIT**
Includes access to the
teaching videos and a copy
of the book.

Additional resources
available at lifeway.com/
revivalgeneration.

Available in the **Lifeway On Demand** app

Stream on these devices: